FRUSTRATION

FRUSTRATION

THE BREAKFAST OF CHAMPIONS

Turn **POWERFUL EMOTIONS** into **CAREER SUCCESS**

VICKI McMANUS PETERSON

Published by Advantage, Charleston, South Carolina.
Member of Advantage Media Group.

ADVANTAGE is a registered trademark and the Advantage colophon is a trademark of Advantage Media Group, Inc.

Printed in the United States of America.

ISBN: 978-159932-601-6
LCCN: 2015934355

Book design by George Stevens.

This publication is designed to provide accurate and authoritative information in regard to the subject matter covered. It is sold with the understanding that the publisher is not engaged in rendering legal, accounting, or other professional services. If legal advice or other expert assistance is required, the services of a competent professional person should be sought.

Advantage Media Group is proud to be a part of the Tree Neutral® program. Tree Neutral offsets the number of trees consumed in the production and printing of this book by taking proactive steps such as planting trees in direct proportion to the number of trees used to print books. To learn more about Tree Neutral, please visit **www.treeneutral.com**. To learn more about Advantage's commitment to being a responsible steward of the environment, please visit **www.advantagefamily.com/green**

Advantage Media Group is a publisher of business, self-improvement, and professional development books and online learning. We help entrepreneurs, business leaders, and professionals share their Stories, Passion, and Knowledge to help others Learn & Grow. Do you have a manuscript or book idea that you would like us to consider for publishing? Please visit **advantagefamily.com** or call **1.866.775.1696**.

Dedicated to the light that shines in each of us.

FOREWORD

Do you ever wonder why some people stay stuck in jobs they don't like, in relationships that don't bring out the best in them, or in situations that cause them endless frustration?

We have all known that person—the friend, neighbor, family member, or coworker who can't seem to get out of their own way, despite the myriad of people around them who are willing to help. You may even be that person, hoping to find answers in this book. If so, **keep reading!**

Several years ago, I was the manager of a global career transition firm. We provided career coaching for more than 700 individuals annually who were laid off from their jobs. They walked into our doors feeling scared, frustrated, and extremely anxious about the prospect of finding new work. And yet, with few exceptions, they ended up getting new jobs that brought them more happiness and fulfillment than before, often with better compensation.

I always think to myself:

Why did the layoff have to be the catalyst for change?

If the layoff hadn't happened, how long would they have stayed in jobs that frustrated and bored them?

Sadly, many people stay far too long. They get comfortable. And in doing so, they miss out on tremendous opportunity for career and spiritual growth, better physical well-being, and financial rewards.

I've spent the better part of my career helping organizations and individuals achieve greater success and personal fulfillment through change. I've partnered with senior leadership teams of Fortune 100 companies and coached hundreds of individuals and leaders. Some rise to the occasion, others falter.

Vicki is one of those individuals who rises, again and again, and brings others along with her. Her passion and energy is contagious, and I am thrilled to see it come through in *Frustration: The Breakfast of Champions*.

If you picked up this book, you may be frustrated and potentially paralyzed in one way or another. Why wait for a layoff or an event that's out of your control to make change in your life? Vicki has created an accessible and pragmatic road map for you to follow. I encourage you to let her words and approach guide your journey from being stuck to thriving in a new and better reality. Let your frustration fuel your action. Go on…it's time for Breakfast!

Thana Sakas
Owner/Founder
Gramercy Consulting
http://gramercy-consulting.com/

TABLE OF CONTENTS

INTRODUCTION

Like most people, I spent many years trapped by my own negative emotions. Frustration, anger, and disappointment held me back from fulfilling my true potential. My journey into discovery of the ways to unlock hidden talents began in 1979 when I took a Dale Carnegie course, "How to Win Friends and Influence People." The legacy of Dale Carnegie lives on today because the message is timeless.

As my career evolved, I sought out bigger and bigger challenges, thinking that if I could just make it to the next level, my problems would be solved and that I wouldn't be so frustrated by other people. Boy, was I wrong! What I didn't know at the time was that responsibility inherently carries with it the unspoken need to improve communication with others. The higher you go, the more potential frustration you experience.

I was also unaware that as a species we are hardwired to notice the negative first! Back in the days of caveman existence, it was imperative to spot danger, so we developed a very strong "fight or flight" mechanism for protection. We also naturally tend to remember negative experiences longer, because it is more important to remember the color of the poisonous snake or berry than the beautiful colors of a butterfly. Negative, frustrating people were simply "being" what we are designed to be. The good news is that emotional intelligence (like physical strength) can be trained!

I was fortunate to have worked for employers who believed in continuing education and self-development. I was given opportunities to step into leadership roles within our company that sparked a genuine interest in helping others succeed.

We were exposed to peak performance coaching, neurolinguistics, and leadership development. As I thought about new work opportunities, I reached out to the training company who worked with our team and gained a part-time job as an event coordinator for local seminars.

That was the beginning of a journey that has led me to create a national management and marketing firm. We've been listed on the Inc. 5000 list of fastest-growing privately held companies in 2012, 2013, and 2014. I was also honored with a Silver Stevie Women in Business Award in 2013, as Female Entrepreneur of the Year.

I share these accomplishments as an example of what is possible when you embrace the frustrations of life—and commit to overcoming them.

As a certified emotional intelligence coach, I have the opportunity to work with people at every level of an organization. Over the years, I began seeing a clear distinction between the few who were successful in their careers and the masses who were not.

The reason most people become stuck along the way and never realize their potential became clear. "Why did you give up?" I'd ask. Time after time, the answer was, "I became frustrated and decided it just wasn't worth it!"

Frustrated, I'd respond! Are you kidding me? I *love* frustration. That is my indicator that I'm passionate about the goal, and I've not yet discovered the right solution. Frustration fuels my resolve to push further, to change my approach, to seek new mentors, to read more, ask more, do more.

I hope that you discover in this book that frustration is a green light. Understanding this one concept will propel you ahead of your coworkers and competitors that insist on viewing frustration as a stop sign, a signal to give up. Throughout this book, I'll challenge you to listen to your emotions for the positive message they are sending and then discover the highest and best use of your time and emotional energy.

> "When I was a child, I spake as a
> child, I felt as a child, I thought as a
> child: now that I am become a man,
> I have put away childish things.
>
> —*1 Corinthians 13:11 (ASV)*

Frustration is one of those childlike thoughts that can be transformed with a bit of focus. Life's journey is a series of solving problems. They can be short-term issues that you get through quickly or longer-term goals that need a game plan. Problem solving is simply the act of choosing a path, making a decision, and facing the consequences—good and bad.

Fear of voicing opinions, choosing a path, or making a decision are clear roots of frustration. In a world that rewards compliance, not creativity, frustrations can run high.

Most people attempt to "fit" into their company culture by suppressing their opinions. Conforming to the "norm" within your company can (and does) kill both dreams and career advancement. Frustrations inevitably build and can lead to one of two choices: (1) accepting disappointment and fitting into a box that someone else has created for you or (2) breaking through to success.

This book will teach you to understand how emotional strength and emotional intelligence are vital to your career and how to create strategies for dealing with frustration and other emotions. By better understanding the choices you make and combining frustration with empowering emotions to create powerful results, you will be able to turn what you thought was negative feedback into positive action and use the frustrations that used to cause setbacks to continue expanding your career options.

Frustration: The Breakfast of Champions is a winning strategy that I've developed as a personal and business coach over the past two decades. Frustration is merely dissatisfaction with your current situation. Dissatisfaction can be the mother of disruption, but it's also the single biggest motivator for change in your life.

If you find yourself sitting at your desk daydreaming of a better job or simply a better relationship in your current company, this book is for you. Frustration can truly be the breakfast of champions! So get ready to turn your daily dose into a positive driving force in your life.

CHAPTER 1

FRUSTRATION FOR BREAKFAST? FUEL UP!

Everyone experiences frustration on the job—it's a totally natural emotion. Overbearing supervisors, gossiping coworkers, unbreakable wage ceilings, ever-lengthening hours…it can all drive you a bit crazy.

But that frustration doesn't have to ruin your life. In fact, you can turn it into a driving force to make your current job better or launch you into a better one. Imagine the frustration of knowing your current career must come to a sudden end.

LIFE LISTEN

My daughter, Hillary, is a bright young woman who recently graduated from culinary school as a pastry chef. She loves the precision of the method and making people happy with sweet treats. Much to her dismay, she discovered that she was totally allergic to wheat. Within six months of graduation, her dreams shattered. Without the ability to taste, touch, or breathe wheat products, her prospects in this field became extremely limited. While gluten-free bakeries are emerging, the job market remains quite small. She had saved a bit of money, and instead of heading back to college, she backpacked Ireland and England, taking time to discover new passions. She came back to a retail job with a chocolatier and began exploring new opportunities to use her natural talents of precision, detail, culinary knowledge, and customer service to relaunch her career.

Have you ever thought of frustration as a positive emotion? It probably seems counterintuitive. Frustration is certainly not an enjoyable emotion. But it can be something positive in your life if you understand what your feelings are trying to tell you. If you start your day with a bowl of frustrations, you could be on your way to realizing your dreams!

You'll soon know how to:

- Understand how emotional strength is vital to your career.

- Create strategies for dealing with frustration and other emotions.

- Realize that the choices you make are creating your career and your life.

- Combine frustration with empowering emotions to get the outcome you want.

If you've ever spent a restless night, tortured by the voices in your head dreading the next day or telling you that you are just not good enough to reach for more in life, I encourage you to dive deep into the chapters ahead.

WHY ARE YOU FRUSTRATED?

In the business world, frustrations are everywhere! Some situations are out of our control, but many can be managed if we first learn why they are frustrating us.

Frustration usually creeps in when…

- You don't have enough focused time to create achievable goals.

- The goals you want to achieve are not happening as fast as you want.

- You feel you have no control over a situation.

You can't accomplish all your goals at once. Frustration often comes when you don't seem to be making forward progress. When you can't focus on your goals because you are overwhelmed, organize your priorities and get something done!

Completing one high-impact item on your long to-do list, especially one that has been weighing you down, can provide the renewed energy to do more. When you are stuck, ask yourself these questions. The answers can help you get moving again.

- Where am I procrastinating? Why?

- What am I doing that is draining my energy?

- What is the highest and best use of my time?

- Which projects (or segments) have the highest impact?

- Are there aspects that can be delegated to others?

It may sound funny, but when it comes to achieving your goals and mastering the frustrations that can get in the way, you can take a lesson from kids.

Think about it. When a child wants a piece of candy or a new toy, he asks for it. He doesn't hesitate.

"Mom, can I please have this truck?"

The typical first answer is no; but children know what they want and don't give up until they get it. They are persistent... some may say nagging, but they give it their all. If they don't get what they want the first time, they change their approach.

"Mom, if you get me this truck, I'll clean my room..."

"Mom, if you get me this truck, I'll take out the trash..."

It doesn't always work for the child, but changing approaches and being persistent are good habits to get into in the work place. Persistence does not give you permission to be annoying! The point is to know what you want, focus on the outcomes, review your approach constantly, and stay the course until you break through to success or find an alternative that satisfies your outcome.

Learn to recognize frustration as simply a communication tool from within yourself telling you, "Hey, pay attention here!" The goal you're striving for is likely something that you deserve and could have. Align frustration with other powerful emotions like curiosity. Then become **cooperative, tenacious,** and **persistent,** and you'll be on the road to making your goal.

WHAT ARE YOU FEELING?

It can be easy to figure out why you are frustrated and take some initial steps to manage those frustrations. The tricky part is taking it to the next level and understanding how you react emotionally to frustrations. If you don't understand your emotions and can't control them, then you will continue to feel frustrated and never get the outcome you desire.

So, when you first become frustrated, how do you feel? Angry? Sad? Out of control? Confused?

Step one is to expand your emotional vocabulary, to describe more accurately what you are feeling at a given moment, not just in terms of frustration, but for all of those "negative" emotions that we experience. How we label these experiences becomes **how** we experience them. When you come up against a stressful situation, ask yourself, "Was I stressed or was I…"

- Concerned
- In need of clarity
- Misinformed
- Time pressured
- Nervous

In order to take control of your professional career, you have to understand the role that emotions play in your life. The simplest way to think about emotions is that they are energy in motion. Like all energetic forces, emotions flow through us and manifest themselves in the world around us.

We've all had the experience of being a little down and suddenly interacting with someone who was having a great day or listened to a favorite song that anchored us to happy memories. The energy of these interactions helped to lift us up. Learning to channel your emotional energy can have a profound impact on yourself and others.

"Emotions equal energy in motion."

—R. Neville Johnston

Have you ever stopped to think about what kind of emotions you experience on any given day or during the course of a week?

Try this exercise to see how your emotions have affected you over the last week.

E-MOTION EXERCISE

List at least ten emotions that you've felt in the past week:

1.   6.

2.   7.

3.   8.

4.   9.

5.   10.

Answer the following questions:

1. First, did you find it difficult to list ten emotions?

2. Of the emotions that you listed, what is the ratio of positive to negative?

3. Which emotions would you consider positive, and which would you consider negative?

The reality is that most people can't list ten emotions. There are probably 500+ words to describe emotions if you get very granular with your vocabulary. Take the word "zealous." We don't often say, "I feel zealous today!"

Limited emotional vocabulary limits our reaction to life and sets comfortable (often destructive) patterns. Common patterns of emotions are happy, sad, angry, loved, frustrated. The real kicker is that "happy" often comes with the caveat of "because." I'll be happy, when…Or I'm happy today because…

This pattern of thinking establishes a false sense that the outside world controls emotions. Throughout this book, I encourage you to explore the concept that *all* emotions are self-generated. No one can make you happy or sad. Life happens, it triggers an automatic emotional reaction based on old patterns, personal beliefs, cultural values, etc; the information is then filtered through internal self-talk, and conclusions are made.

Frustration: The Breakfast of Champions will help you discover how to change your internal dialogue and become emotionally stronger.

LIFE LISTENS

I walked into an office years ago and overheard a group of coworkers chatting. "I'm not talking to Debbie today. She's having a bad day." The comment made me think, "What could be so awful that you would allow yourself to lose something as precious as 24 hours of your life because of a mood?"

I decided right then that I would never have a bad day again. I may have a bad moment. I may be dealing with a tough situation, but I will not lose an entire day of joy because of a moment of bad feeling or emotion. The only exceptions I've found to this standard are times of grief over the loss of a loved one or some other traumatic stress.

Choosing to live in a way that I would no longer have "bad days" started me on the path to understanding my emotions. I realized that most of my bad moods centered around other people not living up to my expectations. As a high achiever I tended to push, push, push for what I wanted. The reality is that pushing hard on the people around me wasn't working. I learned how to tackle that pattern and to put a strategy in place for dealing with these emotions.

It's always about working on yourself. It's never about working on other people.

CHAPTER 2

IT'S ALL ABOUT YOU!—BUILDING YOUR STAMINA

nderstanding frustration, and the intent behind any emotion, doesn't happen overnight. Building emotional stamina is a daily practice. You'll discover as I did that even with profound understanding, you will continue to be hijacked by old patterns from time to time. Don't let that weigh you down. Learn to rebound faster.

The journey begins by discovering and becoming your best. Working toward optimal physical, mental, and financial health creates your base. The next three chapters are devoted to these topics.

Committing to healthy outlets for stress relief is crucial. Without a physical release, emotions stack, energy falls, and healthy eating or sleeping patterns become disruptive.

Ask yourself, "Am I showing up at work as a healthy, confident individual ready to tackle the day?"

There are three basics of health that keep your energy high: sleep, exercise, and nutrition. Show up for work slurping down sugary drinks and being so tired that you can barely get out of your chair diminishes your air of confidence. Supervisors may (wrongly) assume that you are not a person of action and will oftentimes overlook you and assign responsibilities to others.

LIFE LISTENS

Karen was very active throughout high school and college. A cross country runner, she never envisioned herself as being anything but healthy and athletic. As the stress of juggling the responsibilities of motherhood and a growing career increased, her focus on health declined. She was overwhelmed and gaining weight fast; this set up a vicious cycle of self-sabotage. Negative emotions began building, and healthy eating habits were replaced by emotional eating. The wake up call came when her physician placed her on blood pressure meds and cautioned against risks of developing diabetes.

That's when my phone rang. Together we formulated a plan. Her best defense was a great offense! She turned back the hands of time by adopting her workout routines that had given her stamina during college. It wasn't easy getting back into running, only a half-mile at first. Her next strategy was to partner with a friend to put the joy back into working out. A year later she was running half marathons! Better eating habits along with exercise gave Karen increased energy and a better outlook on life. It's all intertwined.

THE TOP THREE THINGS THAT DRAIN ENERGY	
Procrastination	⧖
Poor Nutrition	🍴
Gossiping About Others	💬
THE TOP THREE THINGS THAT INCREASE ENERGY	
Empathy and Gratitude for Others	♥
Physical Exercise	🏆
Restful Sleep	🌙

SLEEP

Report after report will tell you that the US is a nation of sleep-deprived people. The truth is that you can't make your dreams a reality when you keep dozing off at your desk or in front of the TV at night.

Sleep deprivation creates a huge negative spiral in your health. It interrupts your insulin secretion, preventing proper digestion of food and increasing risk for a prediabetic state. Psychologically, things get out of sync, and memory loss and poor decisions can result.

While physical pain can attribute to a sleepless night, stress and frustration are the more likely culprits. In his book *Positive Intelligence*, author Shirzad Chamine reveals that all negative thoughts are self-generated. They do not come from the outside world but rather from our own internal dialogue. He refers to the nagging negative voices in our heads as saboteurs.

We've all experienced the restless night where we are replaying the day's disaster with a coworker or the impact of losing a big account. This is your saboteur in action. These voices masquerade as your friend simply reminding you of important upcoming events. When the dialogue turns into a repetitive diatribe of worry, then you know your saboteurs are once again disrupting sleep and bringing you down.

Here are a few simple techniques to lower the negative voices and gain the rest you deserve:

- **Evening brain drain:** keep a "sloppy journal." As the name implies, simply grab a pen and begin writing for five minutes every thought that pops into your mind. Do this about 15 minutes before bedtime, close the journal, and put it to rest.

- **Afternoon exercise:** time your workout to burn off the day's stress. Be "mindful" during the workout, paying keen attention to the sensations in your body, rather than the chatter in your head.

- **Aromatherapy and natural remedies:** lavender helps to relax your mind, and melatonin supplements may help support the body's natural production of this sleep-inducing hormone.

O **When saboteurs interrupt sleep, begin focusing on your breathing:** 4 seconds in, hold for 7, exhale for 8. Repeat the numbers in your mind as you breath: 4-7-8,4-7-8. Relax back into restful sleep.

EXERCISE

Exercise is an epigenetic modulator, meaning exercise can turn on the genes that code for regrowth of brain cells. There is no vitamin, supplement, or drug that can do that!

Exercise is critical, particularly if you work at a desk, you're a writer, coder, consultant, receptionist answering phones, and you're sitting for hours at a time. As a kid, did you make weird faces and your Mom would say, "Don't do that, or your face will get stuck"? Being in one position for long stretches of time indeed does cause your body to get stuck.

As you lean forward into your keyboard, back muscles are stretched, shoulders hunch, and your belly becomes lax. You don't want to get stuck with this posture! Emerging research shows that sitting can be as detrimental to your health as smoking. I was spending so much time sitting in front of the computer that I was probably smoking a pack a day!

Exercising creates endorphins, dopamine, and all the feel-good hormones. Nothing fights frustration like a boost of energy late in the day. Exercise also decreases risk of cancer, diabetes, high blood pressure, and depression. This information alone should be enough to get you moving! But sadly, it likely won't, because information doesn't change our behavior—emotions do!

Think about it this way, if just knowing something gave you the ability to make great decisions—then why do physicians smoke? Did they miss that day of class?

Getting up and moving increases flexibility and joint health; but more importantly, standing up, getting your shoulders back, and taking deep breaths fills your diaphragm and provides oxygen to your blood stream, feeding your body and brain. It is an essential element of sustaining energy throughout the day.

Ellen Degeneres is known for dancing; I'm known for walking around with my headphones on singing (poorly—at the top of my lungs) to some old fashioned rock and roll. This is how I start my day, boost energy throughout the day, and prepare for speaking engagements. Get silly, sing, dance—move! Songs invoke positive memories that chase frustration and fear out the back door.

"Make taking care of yourself rewarding AND fun. If going to the gym is painful, find a new exercise that feels more natural and you'll instantly have more fun."

NUTRITION

My basic rule of thumb when it comes to nutrition: more than five ingredients on the label? Don't eat it; it's not food, it's likely a biochemistry experiment packaged by savvy marketing experts. It should not be in your body. Think of your body as a car and nutrition as the fuel for your engine. It's a poor decision to pollute and contaminate your fuel system.

Convenience can become a nasty habit. Long workdays and busy lives make it tempting to call for pizza delivery or pull through a fast food joint. For years, I was frustrated and intimidated by everything in the kitchen. I was the kind of cook that could burn water and typically used the smoke detector as my guide to check the oven. My culinary skills didn't come until my late 40s. With encouragement from my husband, and hundreds of hours judging the contestants on the food network, I've developed a few fun tricks and tips to make the kitchen my friend.

Shop once a week: We are lucky to have farmer's markets and lots of fresh foods in our area. Purchase enough fresh fruits and vegetables for the week. Immediately wash them, cut them, and prep them for the week. Throughout the week when you open the refrigerator you'll gain a sense of relief—the prep work is done. Grab a few veggies and hummus and you have a healthy snack or lunch. Olive oil and spices, you have the basis of a quick stir-fry.

Must Go: At the end of the week we play the game "everything in the refrigerator must go." Pretend you are competing on the show *Chopped*, and you have to use the mystery ingredients to prepare the meal (cheat: I Google two or three ingredients I have on hand to find amazing recipes).

Freezer: Really work the power of your freezer, stocking it with quality organic meats, frozen fruits for smoothies. We look for sales on high-quality meat or take advantage of local farmers selling meats and fish directly. Rotate inventory with the goal of eating most of the foods within three to six months.

Pantry: Eliminate everything that has high sodium content (over 500mg), hidden sugar (>9g), MSG, and most prepackaged items with more than five ingredients! These prepackaged items decrease your energy and increase your waistline.

Make Change Easy: If your diet needs a true overhaul, take gentle steps toward better habits. Choose one food group to eliminate at a time (cheese, potatoes, dairy, etc.) or work on making just one meal a day a bit healthier. Start with breakfast, then daytime snacks. Perhaps by this time, you'll be ready to tackle lunch by bringing a healthy lunch instead of eating out at fast food restaurants. You soon discover that you lose weight…and save money!

Find a Buddy: Checking in with a friend and lending support when temptation comes is a huge boost to your success. I've been both overweight and underweight in my life—in both cases, the support of a good friend was helpful.

My favorite food magazine is *Clean Eating*. The recipes have very few ingredients, they are easy to make, and they're delicious. They take traditional recipes like your grandmother's beef stew or lasagna and show you how to lower the salt and sugar to make it healthier. You still get that satisfaction of the taste and the flavor, but you don't have the downside of eating a pile of salt, which increases your blood pressure, or high sugar, which increases your insulin resistance. Super-easy, simple changes can make a big difference.

ALTRUISM AND DISCOVERING SOMETHING NEW

Once you've put your own emotional house in order, you'll discover that contributing to others brings an entirely new depth of joy in life. In my work as a coach, I often encourage clients who struggle with frustration, depression, or anger issues to get out of themselves and into others.

LIFE LISTENS

Bob had lost his business and spent years attempting to work for others in his field. Physical challenges prevented him from being as competitive as his coworkers. Mentally, he knew what to do, but he didn't have the stamina to keep up. The negative spiral began to stack up, and his saboteurs were brutal. He began to believe that his worth as a person was in question. His marriage was on the brink of ruin, and everywhere he looked he faced self-judgment and criticism. After losing his third job at the age of 54, life seemed pretty dark.

This is where our work began. After a review of his resume, it became apparent to me that he had valuable skills. What we needed to find was a way to bring his talent to the workplace without the high pressure of for-profit business.

We began coaching by expanding his self-image. A long walk down memory lane helped him to reconnect with his years of community service and volunteerism. This reignited his passion for service. A quick search of the classifieds revealed several public health sector positions!

We began role-playing job interview techniques and applied for positions. Rewriting his cover letter and resume to highlight his past leadership skills and community activism landed him an amazing job. His new career offered health benefits, a generous retirement plan, and ongoing training. He served in the public health sector for the next decade, ultimately retiring as the division leader in his area.

When life seems bleak, take inventory of all the blessings that remain (health, family, friends, etc.) and look for opportunities to serve others. Chances are, you'll discover the same possibilities as Bob.

~~~~~~

EXERCISE

Opportunities to volunteer and get involved with others abound. I encourage you to take a few minutes right now and make two lists: (1) count your blessings and (2) who you could serve.

I AM GRATEFUL FOR THESE BLESSINGS	I WOULD ENJOY SERVING OTHERS BY:
1	1
2	2
3	3
4	4
5	5

Living in a place of gratitude builds strong positive neuroconnections within your brain. Just as going to the gym builds strong physical muscles, acts of gratitude, creative problem solving, and showing compassion for others builds positive emotional muscles.

"Physical fitness is not only one of the most important keys to a healthy body, it is the basis of dynamic and creative intellectual activity."

—*John F. Kennedy*

CHAPTER 3

BUILDING EMOTIONAL MUSCLE

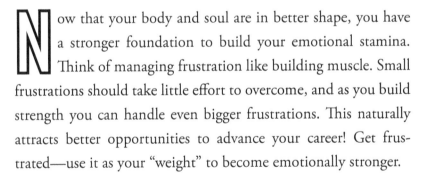

Now that your body and soul are in better shape, you have a stronger foundation to build your emotional stamina. Think of managing frustration like building muscle. Small frustrations should take little effort to overcome, and as you build strength you can handle even bigger frustrations. This naturally attracts better opportunities to advance your career! Get frustrated—use it as your "weight" to become emotionally stronger.

Building emotional intelligence is the toughest work any of us will undertake—guaranteed. Each day is a fresh start, and just like our physical muscles, emotional muscles will atrophy without exercise and focus.

Trust me when I say, I am by no means an "expert" who is always poised and never loses her cool. I am hijacked by my emotions, just like everyone else—maybe more. The difference is *recovery time*. Building emotional stamina will decrease the time that you are derailed and help you recover more quickly.

How long does it take for you to get over your frustration, anger, or disappointment? To forgive someone that may have embarrassed you or hurt you in some way? For many people, the answer to these questions ranges from days to years! Families are torn apart and work environments polluted all because we aren't building positive emotional muscles.

Try these quick exercises to improve your recovery time:

Implement the 10-second rule: Recognize an emotion for the information it is sending and then transform negative thoughts into positive action as quickly as possible. Just as you wouldn't leave your hand on a hot stove, it is unwise to leave your thoughts on a hot mood for too long.

Look for the gift: Every challenge has a solution. Stress, anger, disappointment, and guilt rob you of the ability to look for the opportunity hidden within a challenge. Remember Dr. Chamine's research shows that the upset that you are experiencing is self-generated within your own mind. The next time you are facing a frustrating situation, ask yourself, "What gifts could come from this situation?" Notice I didn't say *will*.

Challenge yourself to come up with at least three possible gifts. By playing the three gifts game, you are giving yourself permission to make up a better probable outcome. For example, when you are stuck in traffic, you have a choice to escalate frustration or look for the gifts; perhaps the gifts are (1) time to think through your day, (2) listening to relaxing music, and (3) the opportunity to think through your morning routine to prevent this stress in the future.

Create sanctuary: Designate a room in your home and times of the day that are absolutely off limits to negative conversations. It could be your bedroom, bath, or dining table. Whenever possible, make a pact to end negative work conversations and dwelling on negatives topics by 5 p.m. Taking this negativity into your home life is boring, disrespectful of others, and extremely nonproductive. Discover ways to decompress before you come home.

*"Take control of your emotions
and the rest will follow!"*

CAREER-KILLING EMOTIONS, ATTITUDES, AND WORK METHODS

I often describe frustration as a "crossroads" emotion. When examined, frustration is a moderate emotion that can tip in either a positive or negative direction, depending on your physical stamina and how you combine other emotions. Combine frustration with active curiosity to brainstorm new solutions. On the other hand, combining it with resignation creates defeat.

Frustration typically is not the emotion that derails careers. An obvious career-killer emotional state is being obnoxious and critical of others. But even that is not as detrimental as less-obvious emotions. My clients are often surprised to learn that I rank complacency, perfectionism, and compliance as the top three career-stalling emotions. When the rest of the corporate world is preaching, "Do as you're told, and be quiet," I say, "WAKE UP, TAKE CHARGE!" Lets look more closely at each of these career-killer emotional states.

COMPLACENCY–BEING TOO COMFORTABLE IN YOUR JOB.

Have you ever noticed how hard it is to get up out of a nice, comfy lounge chair after sitting in it for a long time? Your job can become like that lounge chair. If you stay in it too long, you will have difficulty getting up and moving on!

Creating routines in your job keeps you on task; it feels safe and comfortable. However, if you never take a risk or tackle something new, you limit promotion opportunities. As you take on new tasks, don't be afraid to make mistakes or ask for help. These are signs of growth and show others that you posses a strong sense of self.

PERFECTIONISM AND ITS COUSIN–PROCRASTINATION.

Perfectionism and its counterpart, procrastination, go hand-in-hand in creating a vicious downward cycle. An irrational fear of failing or making mistakes can manifest as self-doubt. You begin to question your abilities.

"Do I have enough information, perhaps a bit more research is necessary."

"Do I have the right credentialing?"

"If I want something done right, I have to do it myself."

Whenever you find yourself falling behind on projects and beating yourself up or making excuses to others, you are experiencing perfectionism and procrastination. Stop yourself immediately and take one simple action toward the completion of the project. Completion (even though it's not perfect) oftentimes relieves the stress and moves everything forward.

COMPLIANT–TO THE EXTREME.

Read here, pushover. While it may be satisfying in the short term to please everyone around you, at some point, you'll need to discover what you truly stand for.

OVERBEARING AND JUDGMENTAL.

This one is obvious, who wants to work with an ass? We all have an inner judge/critic that masquerades as the voice of reason, the logical supporter, or the rule-maker. True innovation, however, comes from discernment not criticism.

Explore your patterns in the upcoming week, and take inventory of times that you are limiting yourself by holding yourself and others to a false standard.

"Those who stand for nothing
fall for anything."

—Anonymous

OPPORTUNITY EMOTIONS

Opportunity emotions represent states in which we do not have the answers to the challenges in our lives. Most people avoid these emotions because they feel "bad." I call this group of emotions "opportunity emotions" because within them lie the keys to your success. Emotions such as disappointment, frustration, fear, and worry are powerful. Let's discover ways to unlock this power to your advantage.

FRUSTRATION–A CLOSER LOOK.

Frustration is essentially the sense of dissatisfaction. It builds because you are committed to an outcome (commitment is great!) and can't find a way to achieve it. The instant you hear yourself say, "I'm so frustrated!" you have found the opportunity for change. Become conscious of your situation and actively play a role in the choices you make.

I love it when a client says, "I can't, because…" Really? Last time I checked, this was the United Stated of America and still the land of opportunity. Who says you can't do what? Most situations, particularly on the job, have a solution or a workaround that will meet the needs of most people. If your needs cannot be met where you are, then take your great ideas to a company that values them.

Repeat after me: **If I can't, I must. If I must, I will.**

Use that phrase any time frustration takes you down the wrong path. It will trigger curiosity, intrigue, and determination. Repetition is the mother of change. Repeating positive phrases, such as, "If I can't, I must. If I must, I will." chemically rewires your brain to naturally follow a more positive path. (Is there a voice in your head right now saying, "I can't remember to do that every day"? If you can't, you must, if you must you _____!)…try it!

DISAPPOINTMENT–THE NEGATIVE ENDPOINT OF FRUSTRATION.

If you find yourself here, then you missed a step somewhere along the way. Disappointment represents a sense of loss. Discover ways to frame this as a "temporary loss." Remember, life is a very long game; looking at any one point in time could make all of life seem bleak.

LIFE LISTENS

Shirzad shared this Chinese parable with our class:

A farmer raised a prize-winning stallion. The people in the village said, "It is good that your stallion is so strong, he will breed and make you much money."

The farmer replied, "Who's to say this is good or bad?" The next day, the stallion was stolen, and the people of the village said, "We are so sorry for your loss." The farmer replied, "Who's to say this is good or bad?"

One week later, the horse returned with a dozen mares following. "Hurray," said the villagers, "look at your good fortune." The farmer simply replied, "Who's to say this is good or bad?" While breaking one of the mares, the farmer's son fell and broke his leg. Naturally, the villagers came to express their sympathies; to which the farmer replied, "Who's to say this is good or bad?"

While the son was mending his broken leg, the king's army rode through the village recruiting able-bodied men for war. The farmer's son was passed over. By this time, the villagers knew the response of the farmer. "Who's to say this is good or bad?"

Be like the farmer. Judging any situation in the moment can cause you to falsely follow emotions (both good or bad) and not see clearly through a situation to the desired outcome. When seemingly "bad" things happen, know that it is temporary and that gifts can come of the situation. When good things happen, celebrate, but don't overestimate the extent of your good fortune.

CONFUSION

Confusion is an interesting emotion. It can be an easy excuse for laziness or a signal that communication is not clear. Laziness, you say? Sure, haven't you heard a coworker say, "I don't understand why we are doing this," or "I'm sorry I'm late on my project, I was confused about what you needed"? Really—confused? It takes fewer than two questions and ten minutes of your time to clear up ambiguity. Don't fall prey to this emotion.

Here's the opportunity; the next time you detect time-sucking confusion within your team, step up with bold leadership. Explain to everyone "why" this task/project is important and how it fits into the bigger picture. Then move them to an empowering track of "What and How" questioning. What can we do now? How can we best work together? What is the best use of our time?

One of the best books I've read on this is *QBQ: The Question Behind the Question* by John G. Miller. In this book, he addresses what to really ask to eliminate blame, victim thinking, complaining, and procrastination.

FEAR AND WORRY—OH NO! WHAT IF...

While fear and worry are different emotions, it helps to address them together. In either case, your mind is typically fixated on something (bad) that has not yet happened. You are likely stepping into unfamiliar territory in your life or expanding your comfort zone in some way.

Projecting worst-case scenarios into your future is detrimental and keeps 99 percent of people from moving forward. The typical downward spiral is to express fears to others who are not in a position to help. By soliciting advice from people who have not successfully navigated your situation, you set yourself up for hearing even more negative opinions.

Break the cycle! The "opportunity" in these emotions is that your mind is providing a check-and-balance in decision-making. Facing your fears and worries head-on allows you to seek proper counsel. Find someone who has faced your challenge in the past and successfully overcome the challenge. You can do this through books, seminars, or personal connections. Tuning out the naysayers oftentimes is all you need to turn your fears into opportunities.

EMOTIONAL STRENGTH

Everything comes back to your emotional strength and intelligence. Emotions, such as anger, disappointment, and failure, when viewed through the lens of opportunity, become the fuel to fire your imagination. Instead of complaining and doing nothing, look at the situation to discover the gifts!

There simply is no straight path to success; if there were, it would be a very crowded path indeed. Life tests your will to succeed by providing obstacles. It's a pass or fail test: view the situation with defeat—game over; view it with curiosity to uncover the gift—you get to continue playing the game.

Two great books on failure and success are *Failing Forward* by John Maxwell and *Success Always Starts With Failure* by Tim Harford. There is a story of how Thomas Edison found 9,999 ways not to invent the incandescent light bulb. He didn't think he had failed all those times, he simply moved forward, thinking that he'd just discovered another way not to invent the lightbulb!

EXERCISE

On a Scale of 1–5 (5 constantly; 1 almost never), rank yourself on how often you experience these emotions. Establish goals for transforming these emotions to create a positive result.

	1	2	3	4	5
Complacency					
Perfectionism					
Compliant (to the extreme)					
Judgmental					
Frustration					
Disappointment					
Confusion					
Fear					
Worry					

Remember, you have more control than you think when assigning meaning to your emotions. Continue to build strength by simply recognizing and naming what you feel.

"An eye for an eye only ends up making the whole world blind."

—*Mahatma Gandhi*

CHAPTER 4

CONTROLLING FINANCIAL FRUSTRATIONS

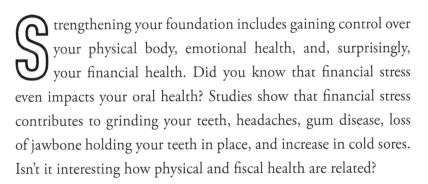

Strengthening your foundation includes gaining control over your physical body, emotional health, and, surprisingly, your financial health. Did you know that financial stress even impacts your oral health? Studies show that financial stress contributes to grinding your teeth, headaches, gum disease, loss of jawbone holding your teeth in place, and increase in cold sores. Isn't it interesting how physical and fiscal health are related?

Far too many people feel trapped by money woes. Starting from the ground up, lets examine financial success habits to eliminate anxiety, worry, and frustration.

Fox Business News reported that 76 percent of Americans are now living paycheck to paycheck, and they have an average of $648 a month left over for savings and long-term investing. Surprisingly, this is not because people aren't earning enough but rather because our standard of what is essential has changed.

Together we'll explore the "necessities" of life and help set priorities for long-term financial success. In a few simple steps, I can help you get your financial house in order, so you can concentrate on better things.

UNDERSTAND YOUR RELATIONSHIP TO MONEY

Do you treat money as an asset or, better yet, as your friend? It can seem like a weird concept. Depending on your situation growing up, you likely internalized phrases such as:

"Money is the root of all evil."

"Money doesn't grow on trees."

"Rich people are greedy or cheated the system."

"Only the lucky get rich."

We have smart money, seed money, spending money, folding money, funny money, hush money, easy money, money for nothing, cash money, petty cash, and ready cash.

We give it, get it, lose it; throw it (away), toss it (around), stretch it, borrow it, bet it, spend it, raise it, and pour it down the drain.

We hope for it, ignore it, and abuse it. We are afraid of running out, so we borrow it, giving banks and lenders control over our life. Out-of-control, impulsive spending is as detrimental to your life as are unchecked emotional eating, anger management issues, or poor health habits such as smoking. Let's upgrade our personal relationship to money and transform it from something stressful into an empowering source of security.

LIFE LISTENS

Looking back, I was lucky to grow up in the '60s and '70s in small southern towns. First on a farm, then in a mill town. My grandparents lived through the Great Depression and imparted the values of being resourceful and self-reliant on their children (my parents, uncles/aunts). Forty years after the Depression ended, my grandmother (Billie-Marie) saved every twisty tie bread wrapper because it was made of metal. The plastic bread bag was washed, dried, and neatly folded for future use. We canned in the summer and ate out of the freezer in the winter. We passed down our clothes to the little kids and dreamed of the day we could go to JC Penny's and get "new" clothes for school. We recycled and reused everything. That wasn't a slogan, it was a way of life, to be frugal and appreciate what you have.

Ironically, my friends all thought my family was wealthy, or at least better off than most. I learned so many lessons from my parents about being a good steward of money. I grew up with the belief that the first 10 percent of your paycheck goes to the church or charity, next 10 percent to savings, live on the 80 percent and you'll be just fine. I was taught to always carry a $50 bill in your wallet, just in case someone needs your help or you find yourself in trouble. And third, never borrow more than you can reasonably repay in a short time frame. I still live by these beliefs today.

HEALTHY FINANICAL HABITS

Financial health increases much like emotional and physical health—with practice and good habits. Here are three habits that everyone can adopt right now:

1.   Tackle day-to-day frustrations

2.   Plan for rainy days

3.   Look beyond the horizon

TACKLE DAY-TO-DAY FRUSTRATION

Living paycheck to paycheck can make anyone extremely worried and frustrated. The primary fear? Overdrafting your checking account, no money for rent, and running out of gas on the way to work! Forget the luxuries—in this stage, it's all about survival. It's been my experience that people with the least amount to spend actually misspend more than those with healthy coffers. Here are three simple rules to nip these basic frustrations in the bud.

Champion's Rule #1: $400 = Zero

Commit today to place (or build up) $400 in your primary checking account. When you go to the ATM to withdraw money, check your balance, if it is at or below $400—you should instantly think *Zero*. Nada, zip, not available, no more money for you!

The reason? Your current bank balance will not always show pending withdrawals, checks that have not cleared, or autodrafts coming up the next day. By depleting your funds below $400, you substantially increase the risk of overdraft. Bank overdraft fees average $35 per occurrence. The $20 that you withdraw today for lunch could wind up costing you $55. Ask yourself, is this cheeseburger really worth it?

Champion's Rule #2: $2,000 = Car

Hoping that life won't throw you a financial curveball is a sucker's bet. You have a 100 percent chance that something will crop up to throw you off budget. Car repairs, home repairs, sudden increase in gas prices, or unexpected illness will tap our reserves at some point. Preplanning can lessen the blow.

When my children were young, about age nine, we started talking about transportation and how every kid wants a car when they turn 16. Our agreement was that we would provide a car, but they had to save at least $2,000 before they could drive it. For seven years before they were able to drive, they saved a portion of birthday money, babysitting, and lawn-mowing, for their "future car."

Here's the logic behind this rule. Most people look at the monthly car payment and say, "Yes, I can afford that." What they often overlook are things like insurance, repairs, and accidents.

The first half of the savings ($1,000) is there to reduce your overall cost of car ownership. Standard auto insurance deductibles are as low as $250. By raising the deductible to $1,000 (particularly for a young driver), you can save hundreds of dollars per year on car insurance. As you continue to increase savings, talk to your insurance agent about the benefit of raising the deductible even further (hint: same method applies to health insurance).

The second half of the savings account is for rainy days. Most short-term impact situations (flat tire, home repair to plumbing or heating, and minor illness requiring extra time off work) can be remedied with less than $1,000.

Whenever you have to deplete your $2,000 rainy day fund for any reason, immediately take action to replenish.

LOOK BEYOND THE HORIZON

I love shiny new objects as much as anyone. As a marketer, I know the ways that advertisers and retailers entice us to part with our money for low-value items. Getting into the habit of asking, "What am I trading for this item? " has gone a long way in curbing my own impulse spending.

When emotions run high, spending can quickly spiral out of control. If we are having a rough day, for example, we often make unwise spending decisions in an attempt to feel better. When you get this impulse, take a step back, close your eyes for just one moment, and dream of a better future. Creating a longer-term sense of purpose will help you look past today's empty spending.

Champion's Rule #3: Today is cheap compared to the cost of tomorrow

The new handbag or shoes, the expensive new "i-whatever," upgraded phones, mag wheels for the car—each of these items carries with it the *retail price AND the missed opportunity for something better.*

EXERCISE:

Take inventory of nice-to-have wants and can't-live-without needs:

ITEM	WANTS	NEEDS	COST DIFFERENCE
Rent/mortgage	Home with granite, stainless appliances, a nice view, no roommates	Two bedroom, in safe neighborhood, convenient to work; possibly take on a roommate	$500-$1,100 per month
Transportation	New car, bluetooth, navigation	Reliable: car or bus, train	$200-$500 per month
Food	Restaurant four nights week/lunch everyday	Brown bag lunch, and eat at home nights	$400-$800 per month
Utilities: water, electricity, gas	Thermostat at 72-75 degrees	Temp: 68-70 degrees	Saves 3% per degree decreased: 3-4 degrees= 10% savings on heating
Utilities: internet, cable TV	High-speed, HD, DVR, HBO, 150 channels	Basic cable	$150 month
Phone	Full data, turbo, etc.	Track phone	$75-$200 month

This short list of life's basics uncovers as much as $1,200 per month in average savings! What could you do with an extra $14,000 per year? Imagine the impact over the next ten years with another $140,000 at your disposal or savings for retirement. I encourage you to look at your own spending to see how much you would save getting back to the basics.

Earlier, I invited you to take a step back, close your eyes, and envision a better future. I encourage you to do that right now—stop what you are doing and give yourself 30 minutes to list out the things you want to do, the people you want to help, the future you'd like to create in the next one, five, and ten years.

> *"If your dreams don't scare you,*
> *they are not big enough."*

EXERCISE

Spend 30 minutes completing this chart:

	One Year	Five Years	Ten Years
Things I want to do			
People I want to help			
Things I want to have			

Wants and needs have become intertwined. By unravelling these a bit you can weave a stronger financial fabric that could provide high-value items in your life. For example: The freedom to leave a sucky job, the peace of mind of no debt, the hope for a bright future for your children, the thrill of taking an amazing vacation—don't piddle it away for a trinket today.

Entire books are written on financial security and wealth accumulation. For the purpose of centering yourself emotionally about the conversation of money, we will pause here. As with every aspect of your physical, emotional, and fiscal health, your gains will be in direct proportion to your commitment of time and activity.

Money is a friend that finances
your dreams. The more successful
you can be, the bigger you can
dream—the bigger impact you can
have on your corner of the world.

CHAPTER 5

IMPROVING RELATIONSHIPS

With a foundation of physical, emotional, and financial health, let's explore how to use EQ (emotional intelligence quotient) to propel you forward in your career. So far we have discovered how to manage your own emotions. That is only half of the emotional intelligence equation. The other half comprises social interactions and relationship management.

There are plenty of opportunities to practice. You will be tested every day, tripped up by circumstances or thrown off guard by an unwelcome comment by family, friends, or coworkers. Expect this—it's called life! Emotionally strong individuals plan for this and continuously build emotional muscles to prepare for life's toughest situations.

A good way to get started is to consider this, *"Who deals with more frustration, the janitor cleaning a high-rise building or the CEO managing the company housed in the building?"* The CEO, of course! Along the way the CEO learned to face fears, solve complex problems, and do so in a way that built strong relationships.

LIFE LISTENS

Everything I'm sharing with you came straight from the school of hard knocks! If there was an Easy Street in life, I seemed to miss the onramp. My own stubbornness and lack of self-confidence stopped me from experiencing a lot of wonderful things. Exercise is one of them. Intellectually, I knew that it was good for me, but emotionally, I just couldn't get my mind to focus. Constant restlessness during workouts combined with distracting self-talk kept me from really benefitting from exercise for years. Try as they might, friends became frustrated with me to the point of just leaving me behind on the sidelines.

My friend Susan was the most persistent. She and I were working out at her favorite gym in Sausalito. She is an amazing athlete whereas I am usually the comic relief! At the time, she was working out eight to ten hours a week and was determined to enlighten me on the virtues of sweat. At that time in my life, I wasn't very interested in the lesson.

Try as she might, I just wasn't paying attention. At first she was frustrated with me. I could see her stares in the mirror as she valiantly tackled the stair-master and I dreamt of Häagen-Dazs. It took about 30 minutes of my disinterested antics before she got off the stairway to hell as I called it, walked over to where I was sitting comfortably on a Bosu ball, and said, "I can't believe you are just sitting there! What type of exercise is that?" I was triggering all of her negative emotions. Then it happened—I fell off the ball, and we both fell on the floor in a puddle of laughter. She cracked up, and it cracked her emotional state.

I think that is how life is sometimes. We get frustrated with others around us because they don't value the same things we value. We huff and puff and attempt to change them—to no effect. Once my friend let go of her agenda and realized that I just needed to have fun while working out, things changed. I admire her, I learn from her, and (more importantly) we maintain our relationship because we choose to let each other be our own true selves.

Social awareness and relationship management center around the concept of being aware of the needs of people around you, then responding in order to maintain relationship. Think of each conversation throughout your day as an opportunity to either build relationships or tear them down. Becoming conscious of your words and their impact changes the way you think and the path you choose to take. In this chapter we will explore more of the mechanics of social interaction and ways to build strong relationships.

CONVERSATIONAL FRAMES REDUCE STRESS

Effective conversation, much like ballroom dancing, is thoughtful and has a designed framework. In ballroom dancing, the leading partner controls the frame of the dance; this invokes confidence from the other partner to follow their direction. Partners are guided by nonverbal cues, such as eye contract and posture, to make the dance seem effortless. Take note—the lead partner is not "controlling" the other person but rather providing the structure for the dance.

The same is true within conversations or public speaking. One person creates the frame, and others respond. Learning to take the lead by preframing conversations, holding to the frame during a conversation, and reframing conversations' wayward chatter is imperative. Relationship management is the art of understanding the frame and creating a mutual agreement about where the conversation, and the relationship, is headed.

Think of a time when you've interacted with a coworker and what started out as a simple request turned in six directions, with no connections between topics. Did you become confused, frustrated, or impatient, wondering when the whole thing would end? If so, you've experienced an unframed, unproductive conversation. In these cases, you stand very little chance of accomplishing the requested task, because there is no clear outcome.

We can all picture a common work scenario where two people are engaged in a mutual project, yet have very different ways of approaching their work. Using the story of Alison and Jake, we'll explore how conversational frames can create positive results.

Alison and her coworker Jake were tasked with launching a new social media campaign for their company. Their work styles are vastly different. Alison is more analytical, focusing on demographic research. Jake is attracted to the fun side of life, gaining energy by linking their company to community networks. Together, they made a great team, but their relationship was often strained.

Jake's social nature made it difficult for him to stay on task, and Alison's hard-and-fast rules approach was a bit off-putting in this environment. She came to me looking for ways to improve the relationship and move the project forward.

Recognizing that her direct black-and-white communication style didn't always help her achieve her goals, she wanted to discover new ways to collaborate with coworkers. I coached Alison to use preframing to set up everyone for success.

Preframe: Preframes encompass information provided prior to the true conversation. It sets the tone, declares the intention, and focuses on the outcome of the interaction. Great preframes address time, needs, and tone.

Alison's preframe: "Jake, I'd love to get your input on the best social channels to develop our message. I've researched the metrics and want to see how we make this project fun and productive for everyone. Can we find 30 minutes about 2 p.m. today?"

Understanding Jake's strengths, she was able to include his perspective into her request. Note that she did not begin discussing the topic; she simply preframed the dialogue and tone (fun and productive). She then landed on a request for time that prevented the discussion from beginning before everyone was prepared.

Holding the frame: Once preframes are set, holding the frame in the center of the conversation becomes the focus. Master conversationalists actively construct the framework. Thinking back to the dance metaphor, you quickly realize the tango has a much different frame than the waltz. Frames can be extremely structured or casual, depending on the situation. Controlling the frame helps everyone understand his or her part in the conversation.

When they met, Alison's first order of business was to establish and hold the frame of her conversation with Jake.

"Jake, thanks for meeting with me. It's 2 o'clock now, let's set a hard stop at 2:30. For now, I'd love to get your top three social channels and targets within those channels. I'd like to see how my research on analytics aligns with your suggestions. Before we dive into the specifics, can you take about five minutes to bullet-point your top three?"

Notice that the primary frame for this conversation is "time." Understanding Jake's enthusiasm for the topic, it would be easy for a 30-minute data session to turn into a 60-minute brainstorming session. That was not Alison's purpose for this meeting. She did two things: stated the overall time and landed on the first piece of information required, providing a suggested time frame for that section.

Reframing: Reframing is a skill to gently guide topics back onto their original thought or purpose. Because people are human, we can naturally go in lots of directions during a meeting. Reframing is a particularly valuable skill when emotions are running high, there is confusion within a group, or you feel that you are on a treadmill—moving fast with no forward progress.

During the course of the social media conversation, Jake became extremely excited and totally engaged with sharing his ideas for media blitz. He was able to communicate the first two channels but got bogged down a bit and had forgotten about the third avenue. Once Alison noticed this, it was easy for her to interject, "Wow! I knew you'd have great ideas! I see we are about fifteen minutes into this; can you share with me your third idea? Then we can schedule more time later in the week to go deeper."

Bringing it together: Using the tools of preframing, holding the frame, and reframing, Alison and Jake created a stronger working relationship. This process allowed each of them to maximize their strengths without becoming frustrated with one another.

SELF-TALK AND RELATING TO OTHERS

As you can see, using a conversational frame is an easy way to cut through communication clutter. Why don't we use this more? Quite simply, our emotions get in the way. Thinking back to Alison and Jake, it's easy to imagine the conversations prior to putting this system into place. They could have easily sounded like this:

> "Jake, how can I take you seriously if you can't stop bouncing from idea to idea. Can't you just focus?"

> "I am focused, Alison! You're the one that's not listening. Social media means connections—to people—and that is messy and creative! Not all numbers and algorithms. You can't put people into a box."

> "I'm not putting 'people' in a box, just the system for measuring response. This is impossible!"

At this point, it is clear that the relationship is on a downhill slide. Internal "self-talk" about what the other is thinking, feeling, and doing is getting in the way of a great working relationship.

> "For as he thinks within
> himself, so he is."
>
> —*Proverbs 23:7 (NASB)*

Controlling the internal dialogue is the first step in creating powerful relationships. Whether you verbalize your opinions or not, your mental focus will change. When frustrations arise, ask yourself a few simple questions:

- Putting myself in the other person's shoes, how would I view this situation?

- Do I really have all the information I need in order to come to this conclusion?

The answer to the second question is always **no!** Regardless of how thin you slice it, there are always two sides to every story. Remembering this helps you to become curious, to ask better questions, and, most importantly, to quiet the inner critic.

In order to form opinions, your mind gathers information from various sources. Your five senses are scanning for visual, auditory, and tactile sensations to prepare for response. Remembering that we are predisposed to automatically travel a negative path is a great start to disarming inappropriate reactions. Learning to more accurately read other's intentions will massively aid you in managing your own reaction to a situation.

LEARN TO READ OTHERS

Master communicators understand that in any conversation there are two channels for distributing information: the words that are spoken and the non-verbal cues. Become a stronger asset within your company by learning to read body language and tonality and becoming incredibly curious about the "unspoken" conversations taking place within a group.

The first step in objective observation is to know that others' behaviors have very little to do with you. In his book *The Four Agreements*, author Don Miguel Ruiz shares this sage advice: Don't take anything personally; nothing others do is because of you. What others say and do is a projection of their own reality, their own dream.

BODY LANGUAGE

Your body language and your tonality betray how you are feeling and whether you are taking a situation seriously. Approximately 55 percent of your message is portrayed in visual cues, about 38 percent is tonality, and 7 percent is the actual words being said. Body language cannot be faked—it will either confirm or negate the message you are attempting to convey.

Facial expressions: are universal language and convey all emotions.

Eye contact: engages others and conveys far more than words can express.

Body movements and posture: leaning in denotes interest, turning away dismisses or diminishes the point; standing erect shows confidence, while slumping shows disinterest or lack of confidence.

Gestures: hand movements and gestures are different from culture to culture and can easily be misinterpreted.

Touch: a pat on the back while giving praise increases the effectiveness, while a pat on the head can come off as patronizing.

Space: everyone has a different comfort zone when it comes to physical proximity. Physical space creates intimacy; be aware of the possibility of making others uncomfortable.

Voice: includes timing, tonality, volume, and pace. Anxious conversations, for example, are often hurried, in a higher tone, and either louder or softer than casual conversation, depending on the level of anxiety.

Practice noticing other's body language and learn to read the secondary channels of communication. Whenever frustration creeps into a conversation, remember destressing techniques and take a step back prior to responding. At times, there simply is too much information to make an assessment.

When put on the spot in a confusing situation, you can buy time by responding this way, "That is a great question, let me think for a moment." This gives your mind a bit more time to process all the verbal and non-verbal cues being shared.

EXERCISE

Building Positive Self-Talk Muscles

Whenever you find yourself upset by another persons' actions, quickly walk through this mental checklist.

When _____ happened, I felt _____ (negative emotion).

1.

2.

3.

This could have meant _____ (positive intention).

1.

2.

3.

4.

Notice that there is space for more positive possibilities than negative emotions. If you are going to make stuff up about other people, why not choose to make up something positive in the process?

Building positive emotional intelligence provides tools to maintain relationships. In most situations, you have an opportunity to step back from the position of having to be "right" and instead ask the question, "Do I need to be right or in a relationship with this person?" I've found most times that being in a relationship is the more important priority. I've also been amazed at the number of times that pushing my point of view would have ended in disaster!

> "Peace is not absence of conflict; it is the ability to handle conflict by peaceful means."
>
> —*Ronald Reagan*

CHAPTER 6

BYPASS FRUSTRATIONS TO LAND A PROMOTION

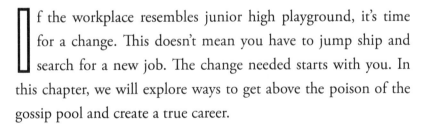

I f the workplace resembles junior high playground, it's time for a change. This doesn't mean you have to jump ship and search for a new job. The change needed starts with you. In this chapter, we will explore ways to get above the poison of the gossip pool and create a true career.

The first step is to stop being an employee and become an intrapreneur. An intrapreneur works proactively, professionally, and autonomously within a company to make it better. You may be familiar with the term entrepreneur: "entre" means to cut away from; an entrepreneur is someone who leaves their job to create their own company.

An intrapreneur, therefore, is someone that uses their talents within a company to create something new or supports creative initiatives. They are self-aware of who they are and how they contribute to their company, and they find ways to create value.

EMPLOYEES	INTRAPRENEURS
Do as they are told	Look for ways to contribute
Not expected to understand the business	Knows how profits are generated
Seeks roles where they don't have to think	Seeks roles that stretch their comfort zone
One out of three employees report work as the place to socialize and gossip	Know that "customers" include boss, coworkers, and consumers and serves all

DON'T BE AN EMPLOYEE

My good friend Ann Allen has been many things in her 80+ years on this planet: wife, mother, teacher, writer, painter, and trailblazer. I recently shared the concept of this book and asked if she had advice for people who were frustrated with their job.

Her response?

"Most people misunderstand their purpose in life. Your 'job' is to continually self-discover. Employment is simply the means to financial security. Whether self-employed or working for someone else, your job of discovering your best and bringing it to the world remains the same."

Ann is right—we need to focus on making ourselves better. We shouldn't be lowering ourselves to workplace gossip simply to "fit in" or prevent being seen as a brown-noser to the boss. According to the Bureau of Labor Statistics, the median number of years workers stay at their job is 4.6 years. Paying attention to your own growth and development has a far better payoff then using your time to correct and judge others. Chances are, it won't be long before the irritating coworker moves on!

How do you know if negative emotions are driving your actions? Ask yourself the following questions:

- Are you guilty of oversharing personal information on the job?

- Do you feel free to "just be yourself" regardless of consequences?

- Do you participate in negative gossip about others?

- Have you found yourself sleeping late "just because" or calling in sick, when the reality is you just didn't want to go to work that day?

Any of these, or variations, are signals that you are showing up as a typical employee, not as a leader, and certainly not as the owner/creator of your destiny.

Self-accountability for words and actions eliminates the need to blame others for your success or failure. Even small steps toward independent thinking build confidence over time.

Companies need great employees; too many chiefs and no one following can be detrimental to efficient workflow. The challenge is not that there is anything inherently wrong with following orders and doing a good job; the challenge comes if you are someone who is frustrated with the status quo and looking for a way to break through to the next level.

Doing a good job and being a good employee allows you keep your job. It does not guarantee that you will earn a pay raise.

SHIFTING INTO INTRAPRENEURSHIP

Listen up! Nobody was ever promoted for being good. *(Read that again.)* You were hired with the expectation that you would be good at the job. Being good allows you to stay on the job, but it does not advance your career, period.

Time doesn't equal value; value equals value.

I head up two related healthcare companies. Combined we employ nearly 60 people across the country. We work efficiently and effectively because each team member is focused on creating value greater than the time spent on the job. We believe that stress is the number-one killer of productivity and actively work to identify stress within ourselves, our coworkers, and our customers.

LIFE LISTENS

Karen and Becky have similar positions, were hired at the same time, and yet Becky is paid 20 percent more. Peeling back the layers of how they spend their time and communicate with others may reveal the differences.

The Challenge: Delayed contract signatures from customers is derailing workflow.

Karen's approach: *"I don't know what you want me to do. I've emailed the contract, followed up two days later, and left a message with his secretary. I'm frustrated and afraid that If I call again, it will only irritate them."*

Becky's approach: *"I had the same challenge and tried something different last week. While I had the customer on the phone, we established a screen share from my computer. I passed the controls to the client, and he electronically signed the contract. Everyone seemed happy, and work began that day."*

Notice that Becky and Karen had the same amount of time, the same resources, similar client situations, yet Becky delivered a better result. Instead of yielding to the frustration and giving up, she got curious, explored new options, and found a solution.

Stress = Opportunity

*The more value you bring,
the more value you receive*

PRODUCTIVE COMPLAINING

The next time you, a coworker, or your boss is stressed, play a game I call Productive Complaining. Gather three stacks of post-it notes (three different colors). Give each person two post-its of each color.

INSTRUCTIONS:

- On the yellow notes—write one thing per post-it that is currently stressful to you.

- On the pink notes—write one thing per post-it that may be stressing your clients.

- On the blue notes—write one thing per post-it that may be stressing the boss.

Gather the notes and place them on the wall or flip chart in these categories:

- Time/Scheduling/Delivery

- Money/Finance

- Communication/Respect

- Resources/Equipment

Your themes may vary slightly, but in all cases you will find commonality in the stress and quickly identify the one or two areas where improvement will decrease stress for most people. Productive complaining techniques allows everyone to calmly and quietly express their stress without fear of embarrassment by voicing their opinions out loud. It also decreases the debate time in regard to who's stress is greater.

TURN STRESS INTO OPPORTUNITY

Intrapreneurs and business owners know that every minute spent on the problem is time taken away from implementing the solution. Viewing stress as an opportunity (a positive gift) helps you to actively engage the creative part of your brain. While this may be easy for you, there will always be naysayers on your team who shoot down any and all ideas. Here is another simple technique that can be applied once you've identified the challenges to shift everyone into positive brainstorming.

Step One: Identify stressers using the game above.

**Step Two: Imagine the solution by
playing the "Yes, and..." game.**

"Yes, and..." is an improvisational comedy tool, as well as a powerful emotional stabilizer for groups. Here's how it works:

- First, state the problem: Delayed contract signatures from customers are derailing workflow. What are some ways we can address this challenge in a new way?

- The first person tosses out a *totally unreasonable way to solve the problem*. The next person says, *"Yes! And what I like about that idea is... AND what I would add is..."*

- Note that the phrase is "what I like about the idea" not "I like that idea." Be forewarned, you will not like or accept all of the ideas. The goal is to retrain the group's thinking away from negative saboteur thoughts into something positive. The game may continue something like this.

- *I propose we express mail dark chocolates with each contract...*

- *Yes! And what I love about that idea is that everyone loves chocolate... AND what I would add is that we deliver these with hot air balloons.*

- *Yes! And what I love about that idea is that we could put our logo on the balloon and advertise to others... AND what I would add is that we simplify our contracts.*

- *Yes! And what I love about that idea is that simple contracts would eliminate client confusion... AND what I would add is that we gain a verbal commitment and credit card prior to emailing the contract. We could fill in the blanks for the client and simply ask for a signature.*

- *Yes! And what I love about that idea is that with payment in hand we could start the work... AND what I would add is that we do a screen share to walk through the contract, then pass the keyboard to the client for signature.*

Bypassing petty frustrations on the job serves to bring the group together. Within a short period of time, these stress-busting techniques can help your team create a positive shift in the group dynamics.

Diving deeper into the problem-solving solutions above, you want to generate as many ideas as possible in rapid-fire fashion, and make sure everyone participates. If time and space permit, get everyone out of their seats, shake your arms, jump up and down, do whatever you need to do to put your body into a positive state before brainstorming. Remembering from previous chapters that emotions are energy in motion, your highest and best ideas will come when you are enthusiastic and your body is in motion.

Work to generate 10 to 20 ideas, then begin to narrow the choices into workable solutions. The intrapreneurial high ground here is to let go of your ego and allow the process to work. Do not get too attached to "your" idea or defend pet projects at the expense of a better solution.

As a team, discover a few initiatives that can improve process, decrease stress, and ultimately provide a better customer experience. One test of solution worthiness is to ask the question, "How will this decision impact us in ten minutes, ten months, ten years?" This helps to identify immediate short-term and long-term consequences of the change.

GAIN THE RECOGNITION AND PROMOTION YOU DESERVE

The number-one reason good people fail to gain promotion is that they become too valuable to replace. Don't fall victim to this trap! If you're the only one who's good at your job, you're going to be stuck in your current position.

When you're on a promotion track, it's because you are good at what you do, you help others be good at what they do, and you have an attitude of service and gratitude that's publicly displayed to your superiors. Begin at least six months before your targeted promotion date to mentor others. Train the talent around you, then bring them along as you move up the ladder.

*Think of your next promotion
as a purchasing decision. It's
not a payment decision.*

When it comes to promotion and pay scale, you will have an opportunity to use many EQ skills: preframing conversations, holding the frame during performance reviews, reframing when conversations are derailed. You'll want to activate Positive Intelligence and keep the inner judge/critic at bay.

STRATEGIES TO MAINTAIN COMPOSURE

Regardless of your level of logical preparation, there is an inherent anxiety built into asking for raises or promotions. A bit of emotional preparation prior to the conversation with your supervisor is critical.

Positive Intelligence strategies that would be helpful in this situation focus on decreasing your own fears and increasing access to the positive mental regions of your brain. As simple as it sounds, you can shift from negative to positive regions of the brain by "thinking less" and "feeling more." Activating your five senses and paying attention to them instead of your fears has the profound effect of automatically putting you in a more open, creative state.

Prior to entering any major conversation, take about five minutes to focus on your breathing and the sensation of touch. Sitting in your chair, close your eyes, take a deep breath, noticing the touch of air as it flows through your nostrils, then feel your back as it is touching the chair, feel your legs, your feet weighing on the floor, wiggle your toes discovering them individually.

Once in your meeting, you can continue focusing your brain in positive direction by wiggling your toes or rubbing your middle finger and thumb together with the lightest touch, noticing the detail of your fingerprints. Your mind has an amazing ability to pay attention in conversation while doing these things. Directing part of your attention to physical sensation (especially during emotionally charged conversations) will help you remain calm. For more on this, I encourage you to read *Positive Intelligence: Why Only 20% of Teams and Individuals Achieve Their True Potential and How You Can Achieve Yours* by Shirzad Chamine.

YOUR CAREER–BECOME "YOU, INC."

From this moment forward, begin treating your career as a business. Great companies are built on a solid vision of how they can be number one in the marketplace and their ability to cultivate great relationships. Your career is no different. Use each opportunity with coworkers and supervisors to control the message, and take charge of your reputation. Using the framing techniques taught earlier, here are ways to take control of the promotion conversation.

Preframe: Address your supervisor, *"Martin, I realize that my growth conference is scheduled in two weeks. I wanted to check in to see how much time I should block and if there were specifics that you needed from me."*

This shows you are being intentional with your career and imparts a positive connection prior to the meeting. Trust me, your supervisor is often as nervous about these meetings as you are!

Prepare: In the time between confirming your review and the conference itself, begin thinking about your outcomes and those of your company. First place yourself in your boss's shoes. What stresses is he or she dealing with now? Is there a way that you can alleviate part of this stress? Are there open positions within the company or a need to create a new position? If so, why would you be the best candidate? Don't forget, promotions are about "purchasing a service" not about "paying a salary." How can you best package yourself to your boss? What does he or she need to purchase today?

Frame: The big day finally arrives. Draw on the experience of sales trainers who know that *"he who controls the conversation—wins."* Start your meeting on the right path by stating your intentions and controlling the framework of the conversation. This may not be your company, but it is your career to manage.

Sample frame: *"Martin, thank you for taking time to meet with me one on one. I know it's part of your job to do performance reviews for all employees, but I really do appreciate this time. I look forward to generating something really great from this meeting today."*

Your supervisor is going to be so relieved. Creating a positive frame from the beginning eliminates tension for everyone and moves you closer to your goals.

Reframes: Your boss also has aspirations. As the growth conference advances, pay keen attention to the boss's talking points, discover what is important to him/her.

A key phrase an early mentor taught me is, *"Listening is not merely waiting your turn to speak."* Sitting quietly, waiting to pitch your ideas will fall flat. Engaged listening helps you to go deeper in your relationship with your boss. At the end of the day, people who are liked get promoted. It may not be fair, but it is the way of the world.

During this conversation, you may need to reframe your own thinking and outcomes in order to align with the company goals. This is simply one meeting in a series of career meetings that establish your path. Putting too much weight into winning or losing the battle will quickly derail your chances of advancement.

The Pitch: Sequence and timing are everything when it comes to performance reviews. Being prepared shows your boss that you are able to think through situations before voicing your opinion. If you've followed the previous steps, you've laid a great foundation. A good supervisor should be curious to hear your ideas.

Armed with ways to help improve the company, you lay out your proposal. Emphasize the areas that you know are valuable to your boss. Keep this brief (under eight minutes, if possible). This tip from professional speakers may help:

Start with a story or analogy to engage the listener. Something fictional or related but outside the scope of your company. At the end of the story, illustrate your point and present your concept. *(Author note: Do not attempt humor in this moment.)*

LIFE LISTENS

Patti wanted to change the direction her company was moving. The management team, in her opinion, had been too focused on chasing industry trends, playing it too safe, and doing what everyone else was doing. She had a plan that was counterintuitive but fairly safe to implement. To set up her point, she shared a story.

"Thank you for sharing with me the points of my job that I am doing well. I will take your feedback and work toward the new goals we have set. In addition to those items, I would like to discuss my long-term future and a few ideas I have for company growth. May I?" She gained permission, then continued.

"Last summer a group of friends and I climbed Mt. St. Helen's. It was a daunting climb, but one I was fairly prepared for. My climbing partner had not prepared as well as the rest of us, and quite frankly it showed. The route to the summit was rocky, gritty, and filled with ash. On the day we climbed past ancient glaciers, it was 101 degrees! Who knew you could hike past packed ice, while getting a blistering sunburn?

'Permit required past this point,' the warning sign (a wooden post really) had said, never revealing the true risk ahead. There are no rest stops, no guides, no way off the mountain except your internal will and physical strength. As the day wore on, fatigue set in. It took 11 hours and 58 minutes, but we did it.

We accomplished something that few people get to experience. I'm grateful for every sore muscle and the days of recovery that followed. That experience taught me that while some things in life may not be easy, they can be accomplished. I am grateful for the preparation I put in 12 months prior to the climb. Even though my friend was less prepared, we worked as a team to make it through the experience together. It is something we will share forever.

This brings me to my point. I feel that sometimes as a company we are not taking calculated risks in order to achieve something greater. I see true opportunity in the marketplace. I have ideas to take our products to a new level. Achieving this may not be easy, but I know with the right resources and preparation, we can increase revenues by 40 percent in the coming twelve months."

(Pause—take a breath.) This is critical to the timing of your presentation. You want your boss to be curious about your ideas and ask for you to present the next steps. Check body language for response cues, are they engaged?

Gain feedback: Your boss will either ask for more information or say something to the effect of, *"That sounds interesting, but I'm not sure we have time to discuss this today."* Be prepared, rehearse these outcomes.

"I understand, this is a review of my current performance, and I thank you for all that you've shared. When could we schedule additional time to discuss my future and how I can create even more value for the company?"

If you've presented the concepts and the boss says, *"Let me think about it,"* follow up with, *"That's fair. This is a brand new concept. Could you share with me what points of my proposal you'll be thinking about the most? Where do you see challenges with this?"*

Assuming dialogue is going well, continue to press for the close: *"Who will you need to consult with in order to make this decision? If you're the decision maker on this, is there anyone else who would need to sign off on it? By when do you think we could make a decision on this proposal?"*

Ending: Always end your meeting on a positive note. Win, lose, or draw, thank your boss for his or her consideration, and say how grateful you are for the opportunities within the company.

The study of emotional intelligence, positive intelligence, and adaptive intelligence has provided me with powerful tools to connect and engage with others. I can think of no better time to put these to use than in a performance review. Here are a few skills to ensure that your boss knows you are listening and are fully engaged:

- Sit on the edge of your chair, leaning slightly toward the other person. As you sit, really feel the weight of your body on the chair; maintaining a bit of focus on your physical environment will help quiet the negative voices in your mind.

- Maintain good eye contact. From time to time, note the color of the other person's eyes. This will help ensure that you are truly connecting.

- Mirror their body language. If your boss leans back, then you can lean back or use similar hand gestures. This creates an unconscious physical connection.

- Be congruent. Align your own body language, tonality, and words to make your points.

Naturally, these are practiced skills; in the days leading up to your meeting, sit in front of a mirror and think about your talking points. Practice maintaining eye contact (without being creepy). Observe your posture to ensure you are portraying confidence. Practice deep breathing to help remain calm should the conversation turn in an unexpected direction.

Practice and preparation are the often-overlooked secret weapons of intrapreneurs seeking to advance their careers. While others become flustered and frustrated, you'll come across as confident and ready to handle additional responsibilities.

MAYDAY, MAYDAY, I WENT DOWN IN FLAMES!

Emotional intelligence is more than prethinking and controlling your emotions. There are definitely times when your emotions will run high; you will be hijacked. Despite your best efforts, disappointment will sometimes land on your doorstep.

Performance reviews, peer-to-peer interactions, and company politics are riddled with landmines. The point here is not to lead you to believe that you can bypass these situations but rather to arm and prepare you for a better outcome.

Imagine the same growth conference scenario with a boss who is disengaged, not interested in your ideas, and has no idea you are craving to do more. Given that this is more than 50 percent of the work environments, it shouldn't be too hard to picture. What do you do in those situation?

First, realize that this is not personal. Your proposal was rejected. You are a business person (intrapreneur) conducting a business transaction. It's never a good business if it doesn't work for both parties. Denial of your proposal does not forecast the end of the conversation.

If your proposal does get rejected or you don't get the promotion, *do not ask why*. Why questions are answered subjectively and bring in too much personal opinion. It is easier for your supervisor to answer tactical, objective questions.

Ask *what* and *how* questions:

1. What could I have done differently to gain the promotion?

2. What talents do you see within me that I should be developing?

3. If you were in my shoes, how would you go about getting a promotion within this company?

If you have a good supervisor, they will be able to put themselves in your shoes and say, "These are the talents I see within you. This is what I would be focusing on and, in fact, the reason I didn't put you in this position is because I think your talents and strengths are better served over here."

When you close the conversation, be sure to say, "I realize we couldn't get a final decision on this today," or, "I realize it's not within our budget to make this happen now, but I really want to let you know I appreciate your time in even considering this."

Rejection is certainly felt deeper than minor frustration. It is okay not to ask the questions right away. Sometimes, you need to let the hurt heal a little first. So give it a few days or maybe even a week and just say, "Can I schedule a time next week? I want to talk about my career path." Rehearse the three simple questions above and come to the meeting with an open mind and curiosity to discover something new about yourself.

INTRAPRENEURS CHECKLIST
FOR PROMOTION

○ **Lay the foundation.** Become the best at your current job. Begin marketing yourself as a "go-to" person who people like to work with.

○ **Train to replace yourself.** Begin training others three to six months prior to your targeted promotion date.

○ **Preframe your review.** Two weeks prior to growth conference, confirm date and time allocation. Let your boss know you are looking forward to the conversation.

○ **Prep work.** Put yourself in your boss's shoes, imagine the challenges he or she faces. Discover ways you can decrease the stress by understanding the company at a deeper level. Get curious about openings in the company or a way to create a new position.

○ **Rehearse.** Success is 1 percent aspiration and 99 percent preparation. Rehearsing your thoughts is the prepwork to successful delivery.

○ **Control the conversation.** Enter the meeting with your outcome in mind. Stay on point and be clear.

○ **Reframe.** Pay close attention to the conversation and the direction your boss is steering the meeting. Align your goals with his/hers. You may not accomplish all your goals in one meeting. Make sure each encounter lays the groundwork for the next conversation.

○ **Present value above cost.** You never want to be known as the expensive employee—but one who earns their value. Value = Value

○ **Positive Ending.** Growth conferences offer a time to present business proposals. Do not take rejection personally. Thank your boss for their time and opportunity for growth.

"A rejection is nothing more than a necessary step in the pursuit of success."

—*Bo Bennet*

CHAPTER 7

FRUSTRATIONS OF A BOSS

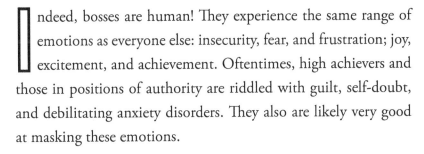

ndeed, bosses are human! They experience the same range of emotions as everyone else: insecurity, fear, and frustration; joy, excitement, and achievement. Oftentimes, high achievers and those in positions of authority are riddled with guilt, self-doubt, and debilitating anxiety disorders. They also are likely very good at masking these emotions.

Until recently, it was taboo to even talk about the high emotional cost of success. Leaders occupying the C-Suite were (are) expected to work 80 hours per week, sacrificing personal health and relationships. Business leaders often portray what social psychiatrists term "impression management," or more commonly known as "fake it till you make it." Hiding behind the mask of success can lead to deep depression, anger management issues, and a host of stress-related health issues. Jessica Bruder wrote a fascinating article on the topic called "The Psychological Price of Entrepreneurship"—it's worth a read.

Business owners, as a general rule, handle frustration very differently than employees, because more is riding on their shoulders. As you are building your career and moving up the ladder, consider this: your manager is likely experiencing a higher level of anxiety, concern, and stress than you! Placing yourself in his or her shoes can teach you a lot.

TYPES OF BOSSES

There are good bosses, bad bosses, horrible bosses (and even Horrible Bosses 2 out on DVD), improvers, advisors, healers, and heroes. The fireball, superstar, visionary, and artist. The stickler, the analyst, and the perfectionist. Regardless of the personality, ultimately you have to deal with them and please them.

Most good bosses adhere to a well-defined track and are easy to follow. The challenge with difficult bosses is that they come in lots of varieties. *By difficult boss, we are not talking about those who are abusive or who condone workplace harassment.* Hopefully, those bosses are outliers in this equation. If you happen to work for someone who is harassing you in any way, and your Human Resources department cannot remedy the situation, do yourself a favor and find another job immediately. Sometimes that is the only solution.

For the purposes of this book, let's simply walk a mile in your boss's shoes. Most readers will experience one of three types of employment:

1. Corporate life

2. Working for a small business typically for the founding owners / partners

3. State, local, or federal government

In the corporate scenario, the stresses on management come from meeting quarterly profit margins, remaining competitive in an increasingly global economy, meeting the needs of unions or employee groups, and balancing that against corporate objectives. (Whew, that is a lot of pressure.)

A second type of companies fall into the category of small business. This ranges from family-owned enterprises to cottage healthcare sectors such as chiropractic or dental, service professionals, such as accountants or lawyers, to start-up innovative tech companies.

There is also governmental employment, which, honestly, I have very little experience and will leave it to the reader to apply the lessons in this book to their situation.

LIFE LISTENS

I recently polled business owners and asked a simple question, "What frustrates you as a boss/owner in regard to your employees?" Here is a sampling of responses.

Overhead Stress: As a [small business owner], one stress that I do not think my staff understands is that my business not only supports my family, but I am supporting eight other families [those of my employees]. If there are cash flow problems, I pay employees and fund their retirement plans before myself. I worry about lean times, as I would hate to need to release anyone. I care about my team and want to make sure we take care of them.

High Drama: I realize it is not always possible to leave your personal life at home, but all day, every day? Gossiping, backstabbing, high-drama individuals are not team players. They end up sucking the life out of everyone else.

Clock Watchers: People who show up late and leave tracks in the afternoon have no place in my company. These folks also tend to be the ones that overstate their hours or take more than their fair share of time off—both a form of theft.

Lack of Accountability, Lies, Lack of Integrity: Hiding mistakes, passing off work to others, lying about results cause high stress for me as a manager. Fact is, if your boss perceives you are lying, then in their world, you are.

Negative, Subversives: There are three types of workers: winners, whiners, and the walking dead. Many people "quit" their job long before they leave the building. Stop the whining! Stop the passive-aggressive tactics. Life is tough enough.

Lack of Respect: Like it or not, your boss is your boss for a reason. Being combative or going around chain of command or over their head is a huge no-no. If you lose respect for your boss, get another job.

While the challenges are similar, the way leaders handle these situations vary. Let's look at a few common leadership styles that Darrell Zahorsky created, called "The 9 Personality Types of Entrepreneurs," to discover what you can do to improve your own leadership skills.

Visionary: Businesses built by visionaries will be based on the future vision of the founders.

Potential Downfall: Too focused on dream, with little focus on reality and action.

How you can shine: Understand the long-term vision and help your boss understand the smaller incremental changes that need to happen today, next week, next month, and next year to fulfill the vision.

Improver: Have an unwavering ability to run their business with high integrity.

Potential Downfall: Tendency to be overly critical of employees and customers.

How you can shine: With every correction, respond, "Thank you for your insight, is there anything else you would like me to do?" You will quickly be seen as someone open to learning, and the boss will focus her "correction" on others.

Superstar: Business is centered on the charisma and high energy of the Superstar CEO/personal brand.

Potential Downfall: Can be workaholic and highly competitive.

How you can shine: Maximize your efficiency during work hours and maintain strong boundaries around your personal time. If you begin answering texts on weekends, your superstar boss will come to expect that you are available seven days per week.

Analyst: Business focused on fixing a problem in a systematic way. Often based in science, engineering, or computers.

Potential Downfall: Analysis paralysis. Needs to work on trusting others.

How you can shine: Show that you appreciate details, and keep projects moving forward.

Fireball: Business is full of energy and optimism.

Potential Downfall: Can over commit and act impulsively. Needs to balance impulse with planning.

How you can shine: If you are easily alarmed by new situations, think through your fears and minimize them before expressing them to the boss. You will likely not be heard anyway, so you want to be very on point with solutions, not fears.

Do you recognize your company owner, boss, or manager in these leadership styles? Depending on their own emotional filters, these leaders can show up as positive role models, insecure, ego-driven, or flat-out control freaks.

STRATEGIES FOR DEALING WITH BOSS'S NEGATIVE TENDENCIES

INSECURE BOSS

These are the bosses who are motivated by fear or insecure about their own standing within the company. They don't want people below them to generate ideas, be creative, or go around them in any way because you might show them up.

Success Strategy: Actively work to make a list of two or three things you like about your boss. It can be small things: she is timely in responding to me, she is the last to leave the office, she shoots down ideas initially but then reconsiders. Push yourself to find value in this person—after all, she made it to this level for a reason.

- Let them take credit. Not all of the time, of course, but give them small ideas that you know that you could execute and let them take the credit for it.

- Be the supportive one. When others in your group or another colleague asks you, "Hey, what do you think about your boss?" come up with something positive. "One thing I like about her is her attention to detail."

Lifting your boss, allowing him or her to take credit for your ideas, being complimentary—especially when you disagree—can seem counterintuitive. Think of it like this, your boss's reputation becomes your departmental reputation. Like it or not, your ability to move up in the company may depend on how top management views your boss's performance. If other division leaders view your boss as weak, then your entire section could be dismissed as irrelevant or nonproductive. Being counterintuitive and finding ways to work with an insecure boss can oftentimes lead to your own promotion!

EGO BOSS

Henry Ford once said, "Companies succeed when it doesn't matter who takes the credit." The ego boss obviously missed this memo.

While this style is different than the insecure boss, ego bosses and insecure ones have one thing in common: the need to be seen as "right." This is the boss whose ideas are the best ideas; he is always the "smartest person in the room." He might listen to your ideas, but they won't get implemented. If they are implemented, the ego boss will have tweaked the idea just enough to take all of the credit.

Success Strategy: The strategy for this boss is to get under his wings and, yes, be a bit of a brown-noser. Ask to be their apprentice, "I'd love to be mentored by you and learn from your knowledge and experience. How could I help?"

Some people are strictly against buttering up the boss, but what can you do? It's a no-win situation. If you want to get your ideas across, it doesn't matter who delivers them.

If your great idea gets implemented, no matter who spearheads it, you still get to work on that project, you get to learn from that project, you get to grow, you get to connect with other people in the company—it's still a good thing for you.

Second rule with ego bosses, don't ambush them. When you go to your ego boss with a new idea, give him time to think about it. You can bet that he is busy and certainly has his own agenda.

Present your plan well. Be passionate about it. Explain why you think it would be good for the company or good for your division, and then ask, "Could you think on this tonight and share with me tomorrow how it could be even better?"

CONTROL FREAK BOSS

These are the micromanagers, the ones who stand over you and scrutinize everything in the world that you do. With the control freak boss, you need to figure out what he wants from you. Hint: what he really wants is for you to follow direction without challenges. To this type of boss, you are just a cog in a wheel. This type of boss is always trying to look indispensable to the company.

Success Strategy: Stay calm and be patient. I realize this is easier said than done! You can start chipping away at micromanaging tendencies by asking soft questions that lead to more autonomy.

> *"Do you mind if I try it this way? If this works, would you be willing to trust me that I could get that done, and I'll check in with you once a week instead of once a day?"*

> *"I appreciate your time and attention. I would love the opportunity to prove myself, can I provide a summary of my tasks at the end of each day instead of verbally in the moment?"*

Publicly challenging their authority or control is asking for trouble (even termination). A direct approach is best handled in private. In a private setting, your questions and response can be a bit more candid.

> *"I feel that the level of supervision borders on micromanagement and is becoming unproductive for both of us. Can I ask what it would take for you to have more trust and faith in me?"*

> *"I enjoy my job and feel that I have more to offer. At the moment, I'm feeling micromanaged and want to discuss this with you."*

CAREER-FOCUSED BOSS

This is not a bad thing, until taken to the extreme of being ruthless and ambitious to a fault. Those who get ahead on the backs of others are often clueless about the impact on others. Complaints, attempts to gain attention, reasoning, and negotiating will fall on deaf ears. You simply may not exist unless you are somehow useful in their pursuit to the top.

Success Strategy: Discover ways to align, to depart, or be content to stay in your current role, as the boss moves up, and you stay put. The best thing you can do is do your job well. Sounds simple, but when your boss is narrowly focused on her own career, you can find it difficult to get things done.

There are ways to work with most bosses. Talented individuals (like yourself) know that there are lessons to be learned in these tough situations. Look for the gifts within the strife. Perhaps you are learning tolerance for others, personal self-confidence, creativity, corporate hierarchy, flexible communication skills. These lessons are typically revealed in the face of adversity, not in the good times we all strive for!

LIFE LISTENS

After college, as I was interviewing, I asked my dad for advice on job opportunities. In order to narrow the choices, he asked, *"Which one would be more difficult? Which one would you absolutely NOT want to take?"* I identified a job that had the lowest pay, was the longest commute, and was totally ridiculous to accept.

"Take that job," he responded. *"It's like eating spinach, if it's on your plate, eat it first, then everything else will be great. Make it a point to have a really bad job early in your career so that you know what a great job looks like when it comes along!"*

I was 20 years old, living at home, newly degreed dental hygienist and totally influenced by my dad. So, naturally, I took the job. The commute was 55 miles—each way! The hours were 7:45 am to 5:30 pm Monday through Friday. The pay was $3.75 per hour (okay, it was a long time ago, and gas was about 75 cents per gallon).

My boss did not realize what little experience I had and was brutal (in my mind) in his expectation. I left crying nearly every day and vowed each day on my 65-minute commute home that I would not return the next day. My dad was quick to point out that it was only a summer job, as I waited for my license, and I had made a commitment. Like it or not, I should stick it out.

Years later, I carry lessons from that job with me. While it was tough, looking back that was primarily due to my lack of experience and not being able to live up to expectations of the job. The really cool part about that office was that it was state-of-the-art. We had a mainframe computer (yup, the old reel-to-reel albatrose that you see in re-runs of *I Dream of Jeannie*), and the office manager was a former model who gave us beauty and fashion tips over lunch!

To this day, I've never had a job as "bad" as that one. I learned a lot about myself that summer, about holding back my opinion and my temper, and about commitment and that you really can survive even the toughest situation if need be.

EXERCISE

Did you recognize any of the traits above within your workplace? Could be with a boss or coworker. If so, take a moment to identify the gifts and opportunities.

PREDOMINANT TRAIT	HOW I HANDLED THIS IN THE PAST	GIFTS IN WORKING WITH THIS PERSON	WHAT I CAN DO DIFFERENTLY

Frustration enters your career path from day one. It is one of the few things that is guaranteed along the way. Whether you are a 20-year-old intern or a seasoned veteran, the way you choose to approach frustration will ultimately be the deciding factor in your success.

Moving deeper into managing your own emotional reaction to life enables you to create deeper, more meaningful relationships. Instead of resisting difficult bosses or difficult situations, embrace them. Forcing yourself to find good in the moment is the most counterintuitive endeavor I can think of. It is also the breakfast of champions—keeping your cool in the face of a storm.

"Emotions are contagious; make sure yours are worth catching."

—Unknown

CHAPTER 8

LOOK
(AT YOURSELF)
BEFORE
YOU LEAP

> "You take **you** everywhere **you** go!"
>
> —*Anthony Robbins*

In working with clients across the country, one of the first documents I ask for is a current resume or CV. This singular piece of paper reveals strengths, weaknesses, a person's level of contribution, and philanthropy.

From 1950 through the early 1980s, the golden rule of business was: land a good job, keep your head down, put in your time, and collect a pension. Anyone entering the job market after 1980 knows that this time-honored strategy can be a dead end. If you are not properly positioned within your company and have ways to continue to grow and add value, your career will stall.

While HR managers are accustomed to shorter work tenures, "job-hopping" is still viewed as something to be explained during interviews. Learning to align your skills with life values helps you to land jobs that will not compromise what is important to you.

Whether you choose to become an intraprenuer within your current company or take a leap of faith toward something new, reviewing your path, the reasons for change, and the road ahead helps you gain insight.

TAKE INVENTORY

Life is more than just a brilliant career (but you already knew that). The quest to create life balance is an area of great stress for many people. While women are stereotypically seen as the ones worried about the homefront, many of my male clients with young families long to spend more time with their children compared to their own career-minded fathers.

A common coaching tool, the Wheel of Life, is great for taking stock of your life balance. A basic Wheel of Life chart might include these six areas: health, faith, family, finance, community, and career. You can create the categories that mean the most to you. Here is a sample:

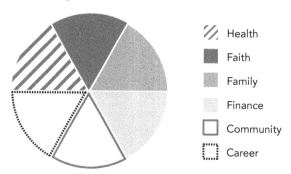

LIFE LISTENS

Alan was a successful business professional, but he felt something was missing. The long hours at the office meant that he didn't have the time with his family that he wanted. His ambition was wrecking his health; it seemed the more he pushed, the less energy he had, and the excuses to eat poorly and skip the gym mounted.

Exhausted, confused, and wanting to get back to the dreams he had in college, he reached out for help. Through some positive coaching sessions, he was able to reconnect with all of the blessings in his life and reorganize his priorities. Within a few weeks of mental exercises and PQ reps, Alan was able to get back on a more positive track. The next step was to assess his time and focus to rebalance his life.

Step one: Create the Wheel of Life. Alan ranked his satisfaction in each area of his life on a scale of one to ten by asking himself questions like:

Am I satisfied with the level of health I've achieved?
Am I satisfied with the personal wealth I've achieved?
Am I practicing my faith?
Am I as connected to family and community as I'd like?
Am I as far along in my career as I feel I deserve?

His Answers:

Health	6
Faith	8
Family	5
Finance	6
Community	3
Career	9

Now, using the center point of the circle as "one" and the outer edge as "ten," Alan plotted his answers.

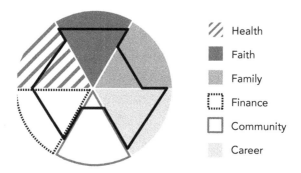

Health
Faith
Family
Finance
Community
Career

It doesn't take a rocket scientist to see that if this is the wheel on your car called "Life," this is going to be a bumpy ride! It's human nature to focus our time and attention on areas of our life that are easier or provide a greater sense of satisfaction. This was exactly what was happening with Alan. His time and energy devoted to work helped him climb the career ladder but perhaps at the loss of connection to family, friends, and community.

NEW PRIORITIES

> "You can have it all, just not all at once."
>
> —*Oprah Winfrey*

Apply the common sense of auto repair: if this were a tire on your car, you would first fill the tire with air and make it drivable. From there, you can assess if there is a weak point or hole in the tire. Can it be repaired, or does it need to be replaced?

This is very counterintuitive if your emotional muscles are weak. Emotionally, we want to move away as quickly as possible from things that bring us pain. In doing so, we miss many opportunities to bring balance and joy to our lives.

In Alan's case, he needed to explore his sense of dissatisfaction with the time he had for his family and social life. Doing this prior to making decisions regarding his career helped him to gain perspective into what was really important for his family. After six months of working on bringing joy into other parts of his life, his wheel looked like this:

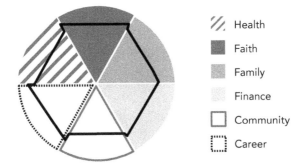

Health

Faith

Family

Finance

Community

Career

Not perfect but a much smoother ride. You can create wheels for any aspect of life that intuitively feels out of balance. Download an electronic version of this at: www.vickimcmanus.com/resources

DISCOVER YOUR STRENGTHS

"He who knows others is wise; he who knows himself is enlightened."

—*Lao Tzu*

My success path has been to play to my strengths and outsource my weaknesses. While there will always be aspects of our jobs that we would prefer not to do, understanding your natural MO *(modus operandi)* allows you to seek positions that play to your unique strengths.

As a coach, I use many tools, depending on the situation. Two of the simplest and easiest to interpret on your own are the Kolbe A™ and Forte® communication assessment. The Kolbe A™ is not an IQ or personality test, but it measures how you do things in four areas:

- Fact Finder—how you gather and share information
- Follow Thru—arranging and designing
- Quick Start—dealing with risk and uncertainty
- Implementer—handling space and tangibles

Kolbe helps you understand why you do what you do. Are you a big-picture generalist that can imagine solutions without a lot of tangible details? Are you fantastic at gathering details, arranging things in logical order, and maintaining systems? These are important distinctions.

While it's true that over time you gather new skills or adapt to various environments, your true nature typically does not change. Putting yourself in a situation where incredible detail is required when you are naturally someone who shoots from the hip will automatically create frustration! Understanding my personal MO has been a positive force in my life and may provide some clarity in yours. For more information go to www.kolbe.com.

The next assessment is the Forte Communication Style report. Again, Forte does not measure personality but rather "how" you communicate with others. The assessment takes about eight minutes and reveals amazing qualities regarding your personal leadership style, helps you recognize sensitive areas that cause you frustration while interacting with others, and helps you to understand your potential reactions so that you can proactively diffuse situations.

The Forte also goes a step further. While your true nature doesn't change over time, how you adapt to your environment will. I call this your AQ—adaptive intelligence quotient. The strategies you've learned in previous chapters provide a great foundation for adapting to your work environment, collaborating with others in a way that decreases frustrations. The Forte communication style report will share with you specifics on how you are adapting and more importantly how you are likely perceived by coworkers. The Forte Assessment is available at www.theforteinstitute.com.

Here's a sample of what you may discover from communication and work-style assessments:

Katie is an "extravert," "nondominant" communicator. People describe her as someone who dresses well and is good with people. She's enthusiastic, outgoing, and friendly. She is also big-picture oriented and delegates detail.

While these are easily observed without testing, individualized assessments share further insight into the types of work environments that will allow Katie to be self-motivated and successful. These include:

- A lot of interaction with people

- Opportunity to make more money and improve status

- Identify with an organization that has prestige and good public image

- Direction as to what is to be done and when

- Freedom from routine

- Freedom from rules, details, and reports

- A generous amount of independence and unusual assignments

In contrast, Katie will be demoted if:

- She perceives that she is not liked

- She has her territory (opportunity) reduced in size

- She does not have enough people contact

- Held to a rigid standard

- Has to create tangible systems

Armed with this information about herself, Katie will be able to bypass job opportunities that are not a natural fit.

LOOK IN THE PUBLIC MIRROR, TOO!

The downside of having a bad day, or a wild night, is that there is always a chance it will wind up on the Internet. Now that you are taking charge of your emotions, perhaps it's also time to review postings on social media.

According to a survey by CareerBuilders, while hiring managers need to be cautious, nearly two in five companies now search social media as a prescreening tool for candidates. Here are a few tips to maintain your great reputation:

1. Privacy settings: Make sure that only friends can see your private posts.

2. Professional presence: Establish a second Facebook presence for professional purposes that is open to the public. Post only things you would be proud to share with an employer.

3. Flamboyant friends: You cannot control what they post, but you need to be watchful and remove tagged photos or inappropriate posts.

4. Be consistent: If your resume says you graduated from Princeton and your Facebook status says UCLA, you'll likely be cut for consideration immediately.

5. No complaining: About your current or past job! Simple posts like "Thank goodness it's Friday!" or "What a brutal week." (even "liking" other's negative posts) can send mixed signals to your current boss and raise flags with a new one.

6. Consider time of day when posting: With smartphone technology, its tough to get away from constant barrage of updates. Savvy employers look at your pattern, are you frequently posting during work hours? Big no-no.

7. Balance: Keep your work and pleasure postings balanced, particularly if you are looking to move up in the company or seek a new job. Too many party shots, not balanced with work efforts, can lower your credibility.

Living a congruent life means examining internal values and aligning them with public perception. While it is not the goal to be all things to all people or to strive to please everyone, taking stock of your public persona can help you align your personal and professional goals.

If you are radical, be radical, contrarian, extreme, and look for industries and occupations that support those values. If you are conservative, be conservative. The point is to take control of your reputation and be consistent.

LIFE LISTENS

April was stunned to learn that she was being fired because of Facebook posts. She earned a six-figure salary, was a leader within the company, and was secure in her position.

The post that terminated her position started out innocently enough. "Thank goodness it's Monday" turned into a three-page rant about work. You see Monday was her day off, she was "friends" with coworkers that she supervised and also with many customers of the company. Coworkers began engaging in the thread, "Why do you love Mondays?" She responded, "Because it's my day off, and I have a break from you people." She went on to disparage customers and her work in general. Not a good path.

April assumed that her First Amendment rights to free speech protected her from consequences. She was only partially correct in that statement. While the Constitution protects your right to express yourself, it may not protect you from the consequences of your actions. To disparage others, especially online, or expressing dissatisfaction with your job can (and usually does) have a very negative impact on your situation.

EXERCISE:

Turn the mirror on your life. Use this checklist to help create life priorities and understand your own innate strengths and areas of public record that may need to be cleaned up.

- Wheel of Life assessment
- Kolbe A™ Strength Finder assessment
- Forte® Communication Style assessment:
- Update LinkedIn, Facebook, Instagram, and other social sites; pay attention to removing any unflattering posts, and improve professionalism across all platforms.

Call a time-out on life, give yourself the opportunity to simply focus on "you." Oftentimes in our pursuit of pleasing everyone else, we forget that "we" are the only person that will walk through each day of our lives with us. It is not selfish to set aside time to nurture your own dreams, your own strengths. In fact, taking care of oneself could be one of the most unselfish acts we commit. In the end, the more grounded we are individually, the more love and energy we have to share with others.

"My recipe for dealing with anger and frustration: set the kitchen timer for twenty minutes, cry, rant, and rave, and at the sound of the bell, simmer down and go about business as usual."

—*Phyllis Diller*

CHAPTER 9

WHEN ALL ELSE FAILS— MOVE ALONG

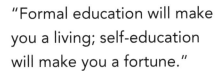

"Formal education will make you a living; self-education will make you a fortune."

—*Jim Rohn*

The big moment has come—the really *big* one: The day you realize there may be better opportunities elsewhere for you. You've worked hard to build emotional muscles and become financially prepared to make the leap. By doing the assessments in this book, you have a better understanding of your goals and your skills—now it's time to make your grand exit.

You're inspired! You have lots of exciting ideas for a brighter future. But here's the rub—you still have to go to work every day where you feel frustrated. Maybe you even hate talking to your coworkers or your boss and are avoiding conversations.

Transitioning from where you are to where you want to be is seldom a flip of the switch. Without an exit plan from your current position and a strategy for next steps, you'll likely fall short of expectations.

KEEP YOUR COOL

Your current business relationships are important to your new career.

The traditional path of exiting a job is to "quit" long before the last paycheck. Disgruntled employees spread gossip and venom in an attempt to feel better about their own lives. After all, misery loves company and diverts attention from personal shortcomings.

This behavior typically leads to confrontations with your boss or a coworker. At that point, you'll likely be given a choice: quit or be fired. What comes next is transition to the unemployment roster, collecting benefits until they run out, then beginning the process of finding a new (sucky) job again.

You've already discovered that *you* are not typical—you are a true champion who's learned to fuel up each morning! Let's discover a more professional way to leave one job and transition into another. If done correctly, you'll take valuable experience and the blessing of your boss and coworkers with you.

LIFE LISTENS

Growing up in the '60s and the '70s in Georgia, my generation experienced massive social and cultural change. Segregation was mainstream. Our school system integrated when I was in third grade.

Throughout high school, racial tensions ran high. Bomb threats, riots, and fights were commonplace. Our principle was a bigger-than-life, African American man named Peter J. Baker. At six-foot-four, his image loomed large in the hallways.

Mr. Baker was cut from the same cloth as Martin Luther King, Jr. Our assemblies were like inspirational sermons. Several decades have passed since those gatherings in our high school gymnasium. Looking back, I wish they had been recorded; his long, dramatic pauses and the nuances of his speeches stick with me. While there is no way I can quote him directly, his sermons would often go something like this:

Apathy: "I can tolerate ignorance. I can tolerate poverty. But I cannot, I will not tolerate apathy!" [long dramatic pause] "I will never tolerate apathy because it weakens your resolve."

Wow! Those were powerful words. How could you tolerate poverty but not a simple emotion like apathy? I had to learn more.

Apathy: a lack of feeling, emotion, interest, and concern. Apathy is a state of indifference or the suppression of emotions such as concern, excitement, motivation, and/or passion. An apathetic individual has an absence of interest in or concern about emotional, social, spiritual, philosophical, and/or physical life and the world.

Mr. Baker was encouraging us to get fired up, to be concerned about social, political, and emotional issues. Discover what we are feeling, and then do something positive to make a change!

Self-Control: In another memorable assembly, Mr. Baker challenged us to take deeper personal control. "In this world you have a choice, you can be a thermostat or a thermometer. A thermometer simply measures the temperature. A thermostat sets the standard. You need to be the one to set the standard in your life. Decide your fate; set the standard high, then set about achieving it! Don't let the current 'temperature' discourage you."

That was 1977. Nearly 40 years later, the lessons remain true. Care about people and circumstances surrounding you, but don't let them control you. The world runs hot and cold: be a thermostat and take control of your reaction. Having compassion for others doesn't mean that you have to get caught up in the craziness of someone else's situation.

SEPARATE FRUSTRATION FROM YOUR PERSONAL IDENTITY

As you prepare to transition to a new position, it is valuable to take time and expand your personal identity. Ask yourself two simple questions:

"What do I do?"

"What am I passionate about?"

You should have two very different answers to those questions. Here is an example from a beautiful woman I met in the Seattle Airport. She worked as a manicurist, but she was so much more. Every pore of her being radiated positive energy.

"What do you do?" I asked.

"I make people happy, that's what I do."

"And you're a manicurist?"

"Yeah, but I'm so much more than that," she said. "I am a dreamer. I have a whole line of natural products that I want to develop. I had it for a while. I had it online, and then I had to pull it, things got tough. I got dreams though. I got dreams in the back of my head."

You could see the spark within.

Being a manicurist, a banker, a graphic designer, or waitress is your work—it is not who you are. I discovered this while working as a dental hygienist. Being a clinician was simply what I did.

Who I was as a person was someone who loved finding creative solutions to old problems. I began exploring this passion. What I discovered was that helping others discover new ways to solve problems gave me a sense of satisfaction, achievement, significance, and purpose. Once I understood the emotional payoff behind my natural talent, I began to discover many new ways to apply that passion.

I worked as a clinician for 15 years before starting my consulting company. In that time, I racked up more than 15,000 patient visits. Here's a little known fact: the average American uses 18 inches of floss—*per year*. Proper flossing requires about 8–10 inches of floss *per day!*

Imagine the frustration trying to get people to floss every day! The task was impossible, so I became creative. When the Olympics came to Atlanta, I started my own "Olympic Flossing Team." It was crazy. I would call patients with poor brushing/flossing habits just to check to see if they were "working out." Turns out, they liked the calls.

I worked as a hygienist, but as a person, I was passionate about health and discovering creative ways to motivate people. As I was considering a career change, I kept that distinction in the forefront of my mind. In my clinical career, I could only impact about eight people a day; how could I fuel my passion and have an even greater impact within my industry?

The distinction between what I do and who I am has helped me craft a career that has national impact. I'm so blessed that our team has touched lives from Hawaii to Nova Scotia, Anchorage, Alaska, to Boca Raton, Florida. Not bad for a small-town girl with a big frustration!

Before making your big career leap, take time to discover what you really want to "feel" in your life. Here is the paradox of life: Success does not create happiness; happiness creates success! Align your work, your efforts with the positive feelings you wish to experience. You'll discover that there are many ways to feel happiness.

BECOME WHO YOU WANT TO BE

> Mahatma Gandhi said, "Be the change that you wish to see in the world." I say be the change you want to see in your career.

If you are thinking, "Someday, when I get the promotion, I'll start acting a different way." Then I have a bit of insight that will massively change your life. You want to start today to become the best version of your future self. Here are three tips that are easy to implement and will prepare you for your new future:

Upgrade Your Style: Take a look around and discover someone who has the job you would like to have. Take note of their appearance, clothing, shoes, accessories, hairstyle. If you are not on par with that style, start to build your wardrobe now. It shows others you are serious and provides a great confidence boost when you look in the mirror.

Practice Relationship Skills: As you prepare to leave your current situation or move up in the company, continue to focus on networking and building relationships. If frustrations are running high, ask yourself, "Do I want to be right, or do I want to be in relationship?" There is no advantage in getting into arguments at this stage of the game.

Be on Point: Continue to discipline your mind to focus on topics at hand. Think of your mind as a computer with file folders. Taking just a second to really identify the conversation you're in and giving thought to how you respond will propel you head and shoulders above everyone else! When you are in a meeting or a conversation, ask yourself, "What folder do I need to access right now?"

- Do I need to be analytical and thoughtful? Access that folder.

- Do I need to be supportive? Open that folder.

SEEING AND SEEKING OPPORTUNITIES

Sometimes, life forces you to make a change. For me, it became apparent that I couldn't sustain an 8-to-5, Monday through Friday work style because of my small children. My infant son had asthma, and I frequently missed work. I needed to create a career that surpassed my income as a dental hygienist and allowed for flexibility in my schedule. Here's how I took the leap of faith and a formula for you to use as well:

Review priorities. My family came first, and then my career development (not just a job) came next. At that time, I didn't really have a particular path. I just knew I wanted a career, something I could control, something I could one day turn into a business, not just continue working for others and having a job.

- What are your priorities?

- Want to build a business for yourself?

- Wish to work for others—which company is the best fit?

- Should you consider a move to fulfill your needs?

Research the Industry: I knew I wanted to create a business, but what type of business? First, I had to discover the needs within my industry. You don't have to start a company to leverage best practices of business owners. Whether you are an intrapreneur within a larger company or striking out on your own, you have to understand the marketplace.

Best rule of business—find a challenge and solve it; find a need and fill it. What problems can I solve? What are:

- Trends in the marketplace.

- My talents.

- Personal work experience.

Seek Mentors: You will be amazed at the generosity of others willing to help mentor you along your path. A great place to start your search is by browsing industry conference promotional material. Top conferences hire the best speakers, leaders in your field. Make a list of people who interest you.

When approaching a potential mentor, be prepared to show an understanding of their work and who they are as a person. Did they achieve something specific that you'd like to learn more about? Being vague or simply asking for a handout will be an immediate turn-off. However, a genuine interest in the field and a desire to learn shines through and opens more doors than you can imagine.

Read: Take a speed-reading class and devour everything you can to prepare you for the next level in your career. I read 85–100 books per year for the first five years of my consulting career! Broaden your horizons to include business trends, social trends, technology, and finance, as well as industry publications.

In his book *Outliers*, author Malcolm Gladwell states that it takes approximately 10,000 hours to achieve mastery in a field. Books (or Ted Talks, online videos) provide a way for you to condense time and learn from the masters who've blazed the trail before you.

IT'S NOW OR NEVER

You cannot postpone this day any longer. You've secured your future position, ensured that you and your family are financially secure, and are mentally prepared for change. Now, you have to tell your boss.

Chances are, your boss already anticipates your departure. If you are a talented individual, they spotted that talent long ago and knew you'd one day find wings. If you are a disgruntled employee, they may actually be looking forward to this day.

This is one of those moments in life where simplicity really shines. A simple knock on the door, a request, "Can I have a few minutes of your time?" Have a seat, present your resignation letter, and be polite.

There, it's done, it's over. You and your boss have negotiated terms of departure and you continue to be consistently professional until your last day of work. Now the negative frustration of this position is behind you, and you are ready to move to the next chapter in your life.

NEXT-STEP CHECKLIST:

- **Polite, professional resignation letter:** Keep it short and to the point.

- **Professionally written resume with cover letter:** Caveat—If you hire someone to do this, proof it well to make sure credentials are not overstated. *(hint: a cashier is not a concierge providing purchasing services for customers.)*

- **Professional headshots:** Interview several photographers, determine the best style for your industry or the position you seek. While employers cannot accept photographs on resumes, you will want to look professional in all online media they may search.

- **Social media:** LinkedIn is the number-one source for business networking online. Update (or create) your profile and begin asking for testimonials, references of your work ethic, and skills. Be thorough in your completion of this online tool and update it periodically. Search the job postings and get active in the forums. These are all forms of networking in the digital age.

○ **Role play interviews:** Whether you are seeking funding from a bank to start your company or interviewing with a new employer, it pays to rehearse answers to frequently asked questions. *Yes, even the stupid questions that clever HR people like to ask, such as "If you were an animal, what would you be?" I hate that question don't you? (BTW: I'd be a giraffe.)*

Begin with the end in mind by staying focused on the career you are building—not on the frustrations of your current situation. This will prevent you from acting irrationally before your departure and, most importantly, prevent you from leaping at the first opportunity that comes your way. Maintaining composure allows you the time to investigate the fit between you and the new opportunities coming your way. While your ultimate dream job may take years to achieve, being strategic with each job change puts you on the path to success.

"Security is mostly a superstition. It does not exist in nature, nor do the children of men as a whole experience it. Avoiding danger is no safer in the long run that outright exposure. Life is either a daring adventure, or nothing."

—Helen Keller

CHAPTER 10

THE NEXT GREAT ADVENTURE

Your old job and bad habits are behind you—congratulations! Now life will be wonderful, no more frustrations!

Spoiler alert. You are about to experience even more frustration; that is how life is set up. But you are ready! You've learned more about yourself and turning frustrations into a power-packed breakfast that fuels your entire day. Now let's keep the momentum going by looking at the first few months in a new role.

> *You never want to be the busiest person in the room, but you do want to be the most productive.*

STAYING CONFIDENT IN A
NEW ENVIRONMENT

Confidence has a cadence. It is neither rushed, nor excessively slow. You never want to appear to be the busiest person in the room but rather the most productive. Feelings are fleeting and deceptive—remember that your emotions are yours alone, only to be shared with those you choose. Don't let a moment of self-doubt become your new reputation.

Taking on new responsibilities, expanding your leadership role, or changing jobs is exciting and challenging! You will have successes and failures along the way, and you can bet that emotions will play a part. There is a high probability that self-doubt will creep in at some stage. Don't be alarmed. This is normal. The pesky inner critic will always be with you. The difference is that you are now armed with tools to turn down the volume on the negative voices and to live in the positive.

Stress in a new career, or as the owner of a business, can come in many forms:

- Rapid growth (yikes! I have too many customers)

- Slow growth (when will we hit targets?)

- Finding the right employees

- Staying ahead of the curve in your industry

Whatever the stressor, tackling frustration and remaining confident in yourself and the outcome are the cornerstones of success. Successful people are confident people.

Let's take an opposite approach to overcoming frustration and lack of confidence in this chapter by looking at the social cues we give off when confidence is low. Knowing that we all get hijacked by our saboteurs, it is helpful to understand how they might creep into our daily life. Whenever we put ourselves in new roles, the opportunities for negative reactions increase. This is common—we all want to look good, especially early on. Self-doubt, embarrassment, or lack of confidence have a few tell-tale signs. Learn to recognize these early and nip them in the bud.

Tell-tale signs that you lack confidence:

Justification: Coworkers and clients expect results, not stories or excuses. Using excuses or blaming others for poor results or delays is a sure sign that you cannot handle bigger commitments. While there is *always* a story about why things didn't happen on time, don't focus on the story. Instead, take responsibility for your results. Others learn that you own your mistakes without excuses. This allows them to join you when celebrating your success! Here's a script to bypass the "story":

"While there is a great story behind the delay, let me simply put your mind at ease, this will be complete within three days. Would this new timeline work for you?" Can you hear the confidence this portrays? Life happens, be proactive in addressing delays, and keep the stories to a minimum.

The other area where stories show up is in accepting an assignment. When asked, "Can you accomplish this?" if your answer is, *"Well, I'll try. If everyone does their part and I can find the research I need in time, then yes I can accomplish this task."*

Let's identify the words portraying uncertainty and justification:

- I'll try

- If others do their part

- If I can do my part

- Then…

Others quickly assume that you don't have confidence in yourself or your ability to communicate urgency to others. Choice assignments will bypass your desk, and you can kiss the next promotion good-bye.

Shutting Down Criticism: If someone says to you, "You don't seem to be on your game today," do you immediately respond, "Hey, I didn't get enough sleep!" or "My alarm didn't go off!" or "It's not my fault because…"? These are clear signs that you lack the confidence to be a better, stronger intrepreneur or to handle even casual observations.

Confident people know when they are at their best and when their game needs a bit of improvement. Confidence includes self-awareness. It gives you the ability to hear feedback in a positive way.

When someone takes the time to share something that I can control or improve, I will immediately thank them! The best gifts in life are wrapped in challenges.

Over-Compensation: You know the blow-hard in the company. The guy (or gal) who is always attempting to make himself look better by shining the spotlight on other people's mistakes. Don't fall into this trap—it is a clear sign of weakness and lack of confidence.

The other type of overcompensator is someone who blurts out all the great things they are doing as a way to divert attention from their shortcomings. *"Yeah, I know I messed up on the project, but don't you remember last month when I gave that stellar presentation?"*

Diverting the spotlight off the subject by either pointing out someone else's weaknesses or your own past accomplishments shows that you cannot handle feedback. It's frustrating for your peers and your boss. The longer you overcompensate, the more you drive away people who are willing to help you improve.

Perfection: Were you that studious person in school who freaked out when you didn't consistently ace the biology test? Frustration happens when we try to reach unattainable goals. Time for a reality check.

Confident people strive for success, not perfection. If they earn a B, they'll strive for an A but probably won't strive to go from 99 to 100 percent. The upside gain is minimal, and the 99 percent result is typically more than adequate for the situation.

I hear the perfectionists screaming now! Yes, I read the motivational poster on the corporate wall. Things like "Water boils at 212 degrees, it will not boil at 211." **I get it, but that statement is about precision, not perfection.**

These are two different things. If your job calls for precision, then be precise. Hold yourself to being precise, impeccable. While this standard can be applied to processes, it rarely applies to human relationships. Strive to hold yourself and coworkers to agreements, not perfection. You'll instantly decrease your personal sense of frustration!

> *Repeat after me: "No one is perfect. In fact, perfection is the curse of forward movement. I'll learn from mistakes and keep growing."*

STAGES OF LEARNING

Whenever we embark on something new, we learn, we grow, and, yes, we sometimes hit a wall. There is a natural path of learning that everyone experiences, yet few are taught to recognize the stages.

Now would be a good time to review your Kolbe™ and Forte® to reconnect with your natural learning style and preferred work environment. Your first six months in a new endeavor will be filled with both positive and frustrating emotions. Understanding the universal learning path will help alleviate stress.

STAGES OF LEARNING:

1. Enthusiastic beginner
2. Disillusioned learner
3. Reluctant contributor
4. Peak performer

You may have heard this cycle used to describe how teams come together. Bruce Tuckman modeled group dynamics in 1965, labeling the stages of team growth as: forming, storming, norming, and performing.

Each stage of learning requires a different level of instruction and recognition. Knowing which stage you are in helps you to ask better questions and gain support.

Enthusiastic Beginner: This is easy to recognize. Things are new, exciting, energy is high, you can't wait to tackle projects and learn! In this stage what is most important is clear, detailed instruction and very little personal support.

If your trainer is being too big picture in the early stages of a new job, ask them to fill in the blanks with more detail. My husband is a master carpenter and residential developer. Early in his career, he hired many subcontractors under one condition: "I will be your laborer so you can save money and keep all the profits, but you have to train me in every detail of what you do. I want to work side by side and have you verbalize every step, every process, tell me why you are doing what you do."

In the enthusiastic beginner stage, you simply cannot get enough information. You are constantly hungry for more and very happy to take on even the most mundane tasks.

Disillusioned Learner: Somewhere between day one and your six month anniversary, chances are you will slip into stage two. In this stage, you start to realize that the task at hand may be more difficult than you first imagined or that the culture of the new company wasn't quite what you expected.

In stage two, high direction needs to continue, perhaps not in micro-detail, but true oversight is still helpful. In this stage, enthusiasm has waned just a bit and self-doubt creeps in. What is needed is direction and a bit of personal recognition.

Be courageous and share with others, "This is different than I expected. As I continue to learn, can you also start to share with me when I'm doing things right? It would help me to get better quicker."

Reluctant Contributor: In this stage, technically, you know what to do. You've demonstrated competency at least a few times, and your coworkers are ready for you to take on the tasks fully. The challenge is, your confidence may be in lag-time. Internally, you are questioning your skills and fear being judged harshly for mistakes.

In this stage, the instruction level decreases, yet your need for positive feedback increases. Again, open up to your boss and coworkers and ask for support. Sometimes just having someone look over your shoulder until you are fully confident is all you need. Choose someone who is naturally positive or request that the instructor primarily point out the areas you are doing well, making minor improvements if needed.

Peak Performer: The stage we all love has arrived. We've mastered the task, no more instruction is needed, and, ironically, praise for a job well done can actually backfire! Think of it this way, as a child we were so proud to learn to tie our shoes (bunny ears, bunny ears, right?) But as an adult, if someone said to you, "Nice job on tying your sneakers," you'd think they were insane; you've been proficient at that for years!

LIFE LISTENS

You may not be old enough to remember the original classic Karate Kid movie (1984). If you've not watched it, rent it and study the stages of learning that Daniel goes through. As the story goes, Daniel(son) is being bullied at school. He doesn't have a great male role model, so he hasn't learned to defend himself. He befriends the ever-popular cheerleader (who, naturally, has an arrogant ex-boyfriend, Johnny). Johnny is trained in Cobra Kai, a particularly vicious form of karate. The tormenting continues. Witnessing an unquestionably brutal attack, Miyagi, the apartment complex handyman, steps in and single-handedly defeats five adrenaline-pumped boys. Naturally, Daniel is impressed and asks Miyagi to teach him.

Let's fast-forward through the movie to discover the four stages of learning.

Enthusiastic Beginner: I'll do anything to learn! Daniel constantly begs for instruction until Miyagi agrees. *[high instruction, low praise]*

Disillusioned Learner: Miyagi's teaching style seems random and not relevant to learning karate. He has Daniel doing mundane, repetitive chores to build muscle memory. But Daniel is frustrated, feeling that he is just being a slave, painting fences, waxing cars—he did not sign up for this! Once Miyagi demonstrates the karate moves he's learned, Daniel settles in for the real training and life lessons to come. *[continued high instruction and praise for learning]*

Reluctant Contributor: The rivalry between Daniel and Johnny continues and can only be resolved through competition. When they arrive at the tournament, Daniel is visibly nervous. He turns to Miyagi and says, "What do I do now?" Miyagi replies, "I don't know, I've never been in a tournament." As Miyagi stands at ringside, he gives Daniel a smile and a big thumbs up. *[low direction, high encouragement]*

Peak Performer: Daniel and Johnny reach the finals. Daniel has been injured by another Cobra Kai member in an earlier round. Johnny takes full advantage, sending Daniel to the locker room, and the physician declares Daniel unfit to continue. Daniel fears that without completing what he started, the torment will never end. He finds a way to press on. With barely a leg to stand on, Daniel remembers seeing Miyagi perform the crane move. He uses this advanced technique to take his opponent down, winning the tournament and the respect of his enemies. High Celebration of the win! *[low direction, no encouragement]*

There's a distinction between things we should do and things we must do. Daniel made mastering karate a "must" in his life. He had a very strong "why" that carried him through the frustration of training and the agony of pain from his enemies. Getting through the four stages of learning takes commitment and is always accomplished when you make something a "must" priority.

If I can't, I must. If I must, I will.

REALITY CHECK

You and I are no different than the Karate Kid. We will start projects, big and small, and either determine that they are worth the cost of completion or not. Getting through the learning curve is step one. From there, commitment, strategy, and cooperation from others, all the things we've covered in this book, come together to help guide your path.

EXERCISE: STAYING ON A COMMITTED PATH

When you realize you are off course, stop, reflect, and ask these questions:

- ○ What is my outcome?

- ○ What are three gifts that can come from seeing this through?

- ○ What are my emotions telling me right now?

- ○ Could my emotional "feeling" of the situation be wrong?

- ○ What am I committed to in my career/life?

Play the "yes, and... game" and brainstorm at least 15 new solutions to your current challenge.

Embrace frustration

and the champion's

life is ahead of you!

FRUSTRATION
FOR BREAKFAST

This book is not designed to have you seek out frustration—it will naturally find its way into your life. In fact, I hope that I've encouraged you to wake up every day with a champion's mentality and start living the life that you deserve. Taking care of yourself, your health, your relationships, and your finances.

And remember to:

○ Face your toughest experiences first
(Dad's advice on first job)

○ Be a thermostat; control your circumstances
(Peter J. Baker)

○ Remain focused on the outcome (Karate Kid)

RESOURCES

Perlmutter, David, *"Epigenetics as Fuel for Brain Health,"* *Alternative and Contemporary Therapies* 19:1 (2013) http://en.wikipedia.org/wiki/Epigenetics_of_physical_exercise

"Exercise impacts brain-derived neurotrophic factor plasticity by engaging mechanisms of epigenetic regulation," *European Journal of Neuroscience* 33:3 (2011) http://onlinelibrary.wiley.com/doi/10.1111/j.1460-9568.2010.07508.x/abstract?deniedAccessCustomisedMessage=&userIsAuthenticated=false

"Stressed Out? Your Dentist Can Tell," Delta Dental, last updated October 2009. http://www.deltadentalins.com/oral_health/stressed_out.html

"STUDY: 76% of Americans live paycheck-to-paycheck," Fox19, last updated June 24, 2013. www.fox19.com/story/22676408/bankratecom-finds-76-of-americans-live-paycheck-to-paycheck

Ruiz, Don Miguel, *The Four Agreements: A Practical Guide to Personal Freedom* (A Toltec Wisdom Book) (Amber-Allen Publishing, 1997).

"Employee Tenure in 2013," Bureau of Labor Statistics, last modified September 18, 2014. http://www.bls.gov/news.release/tenure.nr0.htm

Zahorsky, Darrel, "The 9 Personality Types of Entrepreneurs," About.com. http://sbinformation.about.com/cs/development/a/personality.htm

Bruder, Jessica, "The Psychological Price of Entrepreneurship," *Inc Magazine*, last updated February 4, 2015. www.inc.com/magazine/201309/jessica-bruder/psychological-price-of-entrepreneurship.html

"Science Says Lasting Relationships Come Down To 2 Basic Traits," Business Insider, November 9, 2014. www.businessinsider.com/lasting-relationships-rely-on-2-traits-2014-11

"Apathy," Wikipedia, https://en.wikipedia.org/wiki/Apathy

Bruce Tuckman stages of group development: http://en.wikipedia.org/wiki/Tuckman%27s_stages_of_group_development

ASSESSMENTS:

- www.forteinstitute.com
- www.kolbe.com
- www.positiveintelligence.com
- www.talentsmart.com

GOOD READS:

Bradberry, Travis, and Jean Greaves. *Emotional Intelligence*

Carnegie, Dale. *How to Win Friends and Influence People*

Chamine, Shirzad. *Positive Intelligence*

Clason, George S. *Richest Man in Babylon*

DeMarco, M.J. *Millionaire Fastlane*

Gladwell, Malcom. *Outliers*

Hartford, Tim. *Success Always Starts With Failure*

Heath, Chip and Dan. *Decisive: How to Make Better Choices in Life and Work*

Johnson, R. Neville. *The Language Codes*

Maxwell, John C. *21 Irrefutable Laws of Leadership*

Maxwell, John C. *Failing Forward*

Miller, John G. *QBQ: Question Behind the Question*

Miller, Skip. *Proactive Sales Management*

Robbins, Anthony. *Awaken the Giant Within*

Robbins, Anthony. *Money*

Ruiz, Don Miguel. *The Four Agreements*

ADDITIONAL RESOURCES:

Follow Vicki by subscribing to her blog, or linking to Facebook, Twitter, or Linked-In profiles:

www.VickiMcManus.com

ACKNOWLEDGMENTS

For a new author, putting pen to blank page is a daunting task. My deepest gratitude to Adam Witty and the team of Advantage Media. This book had a rocky beginning, a tentative middle, and an amazing finish thanks to my editor Scott Neville and the team of talented editors and designers at AMG. Together, I believe that we implemented everything this book has to offer to get past the "frustrations" of writing about frustration!

Much love to my husband Pete Peterson, who lost his wife to a keyboard for hours on end; to my business family for stepping up and helping me find the time to pursue this project; and to all my champions who inspired this body of work.

We truly stand on the shoulders of those who came before us. I made every attempt to represent situations in their truest light and to provide credit to those who've taught me so much. If I've overlooked someone, please know it was not with intention. Client names within Life Listens stories were changed, however, the principles of the stories remain intact.

To Sue Babe—For Being My Rock.

ABOUT THE AUTHOR

Vicki McManus Peterson is a passionate businesswoman and a seriously addicted entrepreneur. As canvas is to an artist, business challenges are to Vicki. She finds opportunities where others are unwilling to look—on the edges, in the corners, and in turning things inside out.

She has been honored with a 2013 Silver Stevie Award: Female Entrepreneur of the Year, and her company was included in Inc. 5000's fastest-growing companies 2012, 2013, and 2014.

A native of coastal Georgia, Vicki is married and lives in Anacortes, Washington, the beautiful gateway to the San Juan Islands. She has two amazing adult children and loves traveling. You can find her on the sandy beaches of Kona or at a campfire in a state park; wherever she is, a laptop or smartphone are never far away.

Printed in the USA
CPSIA information can be obtained
at www.ICGtesting.com
JSHW012054140824
68134JS00035B/3431

9 781599 326016